Finding
Redemption
In Everyday Life

Always look for the redeeming moments in life! — Lela Gillow Buchanan

By

Lela N. Buchanan

IPG

Intermedia Publishing Group

Finding *Redemption* In Everyday Life

Published by:
Intermedia Publishing Group
P.O. Box 2825
Peoria, Arizona 85380
www.intermediapub.com

ISBN 978-1-935529-85-9

All Scripture quotations are taken from the New International Version of the Holy Bible unless indicated otherwise.

To protect the privacy and identity of others, some names have been changed.

Front cover and author photos by Sam Buchanan.

Design by Floyd Orfield.

For Cecil, my very own Yogi Bear
Who provided me with so many challenging
opportunities for inner growth, and such
colorful story material, too . . .
Te amo mucho

Table of Contents

Introduction

I like to believe that I'm a woman of faith—strong, steadfast, solid. But I am not, nor will I ever be in my mother's league. Through the ups and downs of life, her faith never wavered—she implicitly trusted in the goodness of God. Fallible me, however, would hit a bump in the road and start doubting. I asked "Why?" over and over again. After a series of particularly ugly circumstances, I finally succumbed to those doubts and lost my fragile, self-absorbed, hubris-driven faith. I reached a point where I sank into the depths of despair, where death seemed more inviting than life. It wasn't that I necessarily had a death wish; I just wanted the hurting to end.

When you're smack dab in the middle of heartache, it's difficult to imagine ever again feeling lighthearted or carefree. A kind of emotional malaise or inertia grips you in its merciless talons and you suffer temporary paralysis. Temporary should be the definitive word, however. If we let ourselves be ruled by our fickle and volatile emotions, we live as slaves to a capricious and indifferent master. Tomorrow, with the nebulous offer of freedom, seems a hundred years away. We fervently pray for release from this bondage of fear and pain, searching for deliverance, not understanding that pain is an intrinsic—built right into the system—part of the journey.

It took me years of railing against the huge injustices in life, desperately pleading for resolution, before the truth penetrated my thick skull. Suffering is meant to be a part of life. Challenging relationships and difficult situations are not divine punishment, unfairly meted out to the innocent and guilty alike.

1

They are, more likely, divine opportunities for inner growth, for strengthening the spiritual, relational muscles that tend to atrophy because we want this life to be easy and pain free. We're naturally lazy and self-indulgent. We may work physically hard at personal fitness or earning a living, and still be lazy at the intangible side of our existence—our relationships—with God, others and ourselves.

Rather than God magically removing the hard people or situations from our lives, then, He asks us to see, hear, understand, accept, adapt, stretch, grow, or whatever it is we need to do to become the best we can be—all under the umbrella of genuine, merciful love. Once we do that, we finally achieve that elusive inner peace our spirits crave. It's not easy. It's not meant to be. But it is worth the effort expended.

I've learned—the hard way—always, the hard way—to look for those learning lessons in my life experiences. Often understanding, or at least acceptance, comes only in retrospect— but it does come. With that understanding also comes the tremendous gift of redemption—the gospel message—in each of our lives. Look diligently for that redemption. Your spirit will rejoice and be thankful.

I *am* a woman of faith. I no longer doubt the goodness of God. Because I embraced my life lessons with a teachable spirit and a wholehearted desire to get this life right, my faith grew up, but it was a long, laborious, and often painful process. Not only does my faith define me, it gives me purpose—a reason to live—and a reason to die. I still prayerfully groan over the suffering I see around me, wishing I could infuse others with the hope and inner peace I've discovered on my journey. I can pray and love to that end, but it's truly a journey of self-discovery and you must walk that road yourself. God will see you when you are still a long way off, because He's always watching and waiting for you, ready to welcome you to the light and warmth—and redemption—of home.

September 12th, 2001

My daughter was working on her bachelor's degree in anthropology and social work—a process that took her seven years to complete. A lot of life happened during those seven years—primarily, tumultuous relationships and all the drama and heartache surrounding them. Out of the ashes, though, God brought a gift of beauty—a baby girl—Elizabeth Grace.

When Elizabeth was a mere one-year-old and still nursing at her mother's breast, the court split this precious life in two, ceding away three nights out of the week to her father and giving four to her mother, as if she were some inanimate object. Unable to comprehend what was happening to her, we watched helplessly as Elizabeth screamed and sobbed her heart out every Friday night, week after week, month after month—for the first two years of this ordeal. We were glad her father chose to be an active participant in her life; we just wished the court had waited to cut her in half until Elizabeth was old enough to understand that separation was not forever.

I was babysitting even then—always, it seems. *No babies today*, I wrote in my journal on September 13, 2001, then continued . . . *Two days ago, 9-11-01, terrorists attacked the U.S. . . . monumental devastation . . . looks like a war zone with thousands of people unaccounted for . . . the TV showed film of people celebrating in the streets of Palestine—it's hard to understand that kind of hate—rejoicing in the death of so many innocent people . . .*

But, then, there was also this . . . *must record an "other worldly" experience of Elizabeth's—yesterday [September 12], while pushing her in the stroller [back up our road], she kept staring intently up into the sky—the only visible entity was a faded sliver of moon—on the way back, she turned around [in the stroller] so she could continue to stare up at the sky— suddenly she said, "Hi"—shortly afterwards she waved and smiled, several times—I kept stopping to look—all I saw was the faded sliver of moon in a bright, completely cloudless blue sky—I guess she saw her angels . . .*

My daughter had a similar experience about that same time with Elizabeth, with Elizabeth staring up into the sky, smiling and waving, except she also lifted her arms up, as if saying, "Take me," just as a small child often does to a safe, loving adult, and just as my almost ninety-two-year-old mother did on her deathbed. Interesting to note that both ends of the life spectrum "saw" some desirable "other" and asked to be taken up into their arms, isn't it?

Elizabeth was eighteen months old that day. Whatever she saw did not frighten her, rather, she very obviously felt a powerful attraction to her invisible visitors. For the entire walk, she stared up into the sky, mesmerized by something hidden to my jaded, skeptical, cynical, distracted, mature eyes. I am pleased to believe that the sky was filled with angels: maybe warm, comforting, ministering spirits of our ancestors who had "crossed over" to the other side; possibly my beautiful niece, Lisa, who had seemed to have had some ineffable, spiritual connection to the infant Elizabeth, and who had been tragically killed in a car accident a few months prior, leaving behind a grieving husband, three young children and loving parents;

or, perhaps, Elizabeth saw a heavenly host of those who had suffered a sudden, horrific death a few brief hours earlier at the hands of men motivated by evil intent, now "fully knowing" and aware from their ethereal vantage point of a suffering little person just beginning her life's journey—a little person who needed to see she was surrounded by goodness.

I once read this true story: a farmer surveying his fire-ravaged farm kicked an unidentifiable clump of something with his boot, only to have several little chicks scamper out from under it. The "clump?" The charred remains of the mother hen.

Hope—beauty—goodness—life—the manifestation of love— all transcendent consequences rising from the ashes of evil, hate, despair, ugliness, destruction, and, even death.

A Tap on My Shoulder

There are moments in our lives that cannot be pigeonholed in some logical category. We can't always add two plus two and come up with four. Our natural hubris cherishes the idea that we are the masters of our own fate, and to some small degree that's true. Most of us have the freedom to choose our careers, our significant others and whether or not we want to have children. Even in the circumstances where we cannot choose, however, we still have the privilege of choosing our attitude—to look for the positive or wallow in self-pity. I remember reading this quote in one of John Powell's wonderful books: *Two men looked out from behind prison bars; one saw mud, the other stars.*

Regardless of how we view life, I honestly believe that there are often unfathomable moments outside our understanding or control, reminders that a greater power exists and may choose to serendipitously reveal a glimpse of another concurrent reality. The Irish call those glimpses "thin places" where the two realities briefly and/or visibly intersect. I call them, "Bethel moments" and I've been privileged to experience many of them through the years.

There's a story in the Bible about a very fallible man named Jacob. On Jacob's journey to his uncle's home, he stops for the night, and as he's sleeping, dreams of a stairway between heaven and earth with angels "ascending and descending on it." God, himself, stands above and promises Jacob a rich heritage. "I am with you and will watch over you wherever you go," God assures Jacob. Jacob recognizes the sacred significance of the moment, commemorating it by erecting a pillar of stone, anointing it with oil and naming it "Bethel," which means the house of God, the gate of heaven. Jesus refers to himself as that stairway between heaven and earth in the Gospel of John.

Those "thin places" or "Bethel moments" offer sacred glimpses into the invisible dimension—they are holy places, infinitesimal encounters, tiny tears in the curtain between the material, tangible world and the spiritual one, and, I believe, our lives are filled with them.

One of those indescribable moments, for me, occurred on a trip we took many years ago. We've enjoyed seeing a few of the magnificent natural wonders in this beautiful land of ours. One of the most spectacular of those wonders—Niagara Falls—is less than a day's ride north. I've actually been there twice, both times viewing those weeping waterfalls through the mist of my own tears.

When Cecil and I first got married, he was an angry man—consumed with anger. Every life situation, every word you spoke—or didn't speak, every dime you spent, every job you did—or didn't do ignited a potential wildfire, sparked by the tiniest ember and fanned by the slightest breeze. Survival was achieved by how fast and efficiently you could quench that fire. I poured pitchers and buckets and giant vats of water on those flames, not yet realizing that I was merely dousing surface flames; that the real fire raged deep within. He was angry at his beginnings—primarily at an authoritarian father, "the old man" who selfishly deprived his family of love, physical necessities and personal validation. I thought it was me. I apologized for everything—my inadvertent mistakes, the mistakes of others' and even his mistakes. I took the blame for it all—and he let me. His emotional well was so dry, he actually was incapable of accepting responsibility for life's various insufficiencies or imperfections—his inner emotional desert dictated necessary transference to others. Others—we—specifically, me—were the cause of all his discontent and unhappiness.

A mere three years into our marriage Cecil and I took a short trip to see Niagara Falls. I wore my sunglasses the entire weekend—indoors and out; I couldn't stop crying. We were supposed to be celebrating our anniversary but we had nothing to celebrate. A charismatic young usurper had interrupted any possibility for domestic harmony. I was heartbroken and he didn't seem to care. I couldn't wait for our little trip to be over, to escape the close proximity of a man who I loved that didn't love me in return—not at the time, anyway.

Constantly living with such volatility, my tears began to dry up and Cecil nicknamed me "Old Stone Face." The tears were still there, of course, you just had to drill really deep through hard rock to find them. I emotionally retreated to an inner sanctuary, carefully guarding the minuscule spark of life that stubbornly refused to give up and die.

Several years later we would make a return trip to Niagara Falls, this time with three of our collective five children: Aaron, Andrea, and Sarah. Unfortunately, even with the buffer of the kids, we were not a unified pair. Once again, an insidious third party had created marital discord, adding to Cecil's always present aggravation with his family. But Cecil didn't need a reason to be angry—it was still a way of life for him—and—he *was* angry. So much so at that time, we all felt afraid. Those of us who loved him most were invariably the target for his frustration or anger—others rarely saw even a slight hint of his omnipresent hostility. Although he never hit me, nor did he use addictive substances, his anger was an ugly potent weapon, made all the more powerful by my tremendous love and desire to please him.

It's not surprising that I wished, once again, for this family "treat" to be over. The tension was palpable; none of us—including Cecil—were having a good time. As we finally began our trip home, approximately an eight hour ride, Aaron and Andrea dozed in the back seat, thankfully escaping the unhappiness of the moment. Sarah, who was about six or seven, sat in the front, sandwiched between Cecil and me. (Prior to the stringent seating rules for children.) The deadly quietness of oppressive fear filled our car—no laughter, no songs, no cheerful chatter. As I sat wrapped in loneliness and grief, I suddenly felt a firm tap on my shoulder. I glanced around to see which of the kids had tapped me; what they might possibly want but were most likely too afraid to audibly express. They were both asleep. I shrugged it off, thinking it had to be my over-active imagination at work.

A second tap came in a few short minutes, stronger than the first. I turned around and spoke sharply to the kids, disturbing their slumber, and they protested their innocence. I knew, then, that an invisible hand had touched me; I just didn't know why. I shut my mouth, not wanting to audibly explore the incident with a hostile adult, silently pondering the implications, but innately reassured, nonetheless.

I wasn't smart enough or tuned in sufficiently to the spiritual reality to grasp the significance of that ineffable touch. It was not a gentle, feather caress. Rather, the hand that tapped me on the shoulder did so with strength and firmness and purpose—it momentarily stung—enough to get my attention. Those few brief moments are the only memory I've retained of that entire trip.

We arrived home safely, grateful for traveling mercies, celebrating the end of our little vacation. And we were all anxious to return to our daily routines, routines that precluded too much togetherness. At the first opportunity, I shared that supernatural moment with my mother. She wasn't surprised. "I knew something was wrong," she said with a mother's intrinsic intuition. "I was fervently praying that very morning for your safety—specifically that guardian angels would be watching over you."

I still don't know exactly why I received those two taps on my shoulder that day. What I do know? For much of his life, my husband had nurtured and protected his anger as if it were all that stood between him and annihilation. He had sealed it in an impenetrable vault—Fort Knox—his treasure secured under lock and alarms, patrolled by armed guards and attack dogs. That toxic anger began slowly seeping out of the vessel he had obstinately kept it stored in all those years—like molasses in January. As his resentment started to fade, his personal accountability began increasing by barely imperceptible, miniscule inches. And, as his anger abated and accountability grew, my personal martyrdom—that "poor me" perpetual victim mentality started to dissipate, too. "Don't blame me for that," I'd find myself bravely stating, and we'd both laugh. The lopsided playing field finally began leveling off. Faith, perseverance, transparency, mercy and love are efficacious weapons to wield whatever reality you're in.

You may find it in a moment. It may be a very long time coming—perhaps, a lifetime—but redemption will come.

Goin' Fishin'

Although my husband enjoys outdoor activities like hunting and fishing, they have never really appealed to me. Not that I'm one of those flaming "animal rights" advocates who worry more about the rights of fish or pigeons than they do the unborn or elderly, I'm just not stimulated by the act of killing—ants, spiders and other creepy-crawly critters excluded. I might feel a momentary twinge as I firmly smash a spider flat as a pancake, but more likely, I only feel relief that a potential predator has been successfully transported to critter heaven.

I'm not totally unfamiliar with the art of fishing. Most of my formative years were spent in the country, first on a farm that had several small ponds, a tiny stream, and a little swamp, and then later, after my father's untimely death, near a larger stream that meandered through the valley where we lived. I had two older brothers and a maternal grandfather who all enjoyed fishing on occasion, and I, too, as a child had used the old stick with a bent straight pin as a hook, worm attached as bait, to catch a couple of "sunnies" and "bluegills" under the tutelage of my older siblings. For me, however, by the time I hit adolescence, fishing had been relegated to strictly "a guy thing."

Years later, I married a charismatic alpha male, who, although he was almost thirty years old, had not yet learned to laugh—especially not at himself, or the ironies of daily life, a critical ingredient to successfully surviving family life. Shortly into our union we received an invitation to go fishing at a friend's parents' farm. "Bring the kids," Duane offered. We had a blended family of his and hers that would soon become "and theirs" and we took our two young daughters along, Shelly and AndiBeth. Cecil had always enjoyed fishing, especially with a buddy, but the pressures of providing for his family didn't allow him much time for extracurricular activities. He worked hard, and he was really looking forward to this expedition—we were goin' fishin'!!

One beautiful Saturday afternoon, Cecil loaded up his family and all his fishing equipment and we traveled several miles to meet our friends, Duane and Carole and their son, Nathan, at her parents' pond. Cecil patiently sat his three girls up with fishing poles, baited the hooks for us, gave us some basic instructions, and left us to it before addressing his own gear. He didn't even have his pole baited when Shelly got a hit. "Daddy," she called excitedly, "I caught a fish."

Cecil dropped everything and ran to help her out. "Good job," he said. "Keep up the good work." He removed the fish, baited the hook, and hurried back to his own gear. About ready to find his spot—the perfect spot for optimal fishing, AndiBeth began struggling with her pole.

"I think I've got a bite," she said a little nervously. She's extremely cautious and fearful by nature and not quite sure how she felt about this adventure. Cecil put his pole down and scurried to her side.

"That's a beauty," he said as he removed the fish, baited the hook and returned to his task.

Immediately my line started moving. "Hey, Cecil, I've got one," I called enthusiastically. "I'm gonna need some assistance over here. You don't expect me to handle these slimy critters by myself, do you?" I asked my husband ingenuously, trying to add a little humor to the moment. He didn't hurry this time, and he didn't laugh, but he did graciously remove the fish and bait the hook for me once again.

He just managed to get his line in the water before hearing, "Daddy, can you help me?" Drop the pole, remove the fish, bait the hook.

"I've got a fish. I've got a fish," Shelly yelled. Drop everything, remove fish, bait hook.

Two voices simultaneously called, "Daddy."

"Cecil," I yelled.

"Can you help me, Daddy?"

"Daddy."

Drop—remove—bait—around and around that pond Cecil trotted, removing the fish and baiting the hooks—silently, now—there was no more praise or encouragement forthcoming. In our excitement, however, we didn't notice.

What a grand adventure this was. Carole's parents had stocked the pond and the fish were hitting steadily from every direction. No sooner did our line hit the water, than a hungry fish hit our line. It couldn't get any better than this, could it? How wonderful that our family could experience such a satisfying Saturday afternoon—making good memories, memories to treasure forever.

My line began pulling fiercely. It looked as if I'd caught a big one. "Cecil," I called, my heart pounding thunderously. "I think I've got a big one on my line." He didn't seem to hear me. I raised my voice and called again, "Would you help me, Cecil? Please? I need your help." He made his way around the pond slowly, as if he were dragging a heavy load. Sure enough, I'd caught a big one—easily a foot long, the granddaddy of the pond. I was beaming with pride, waiting for the praise I rightly deserved for my expertise at this craft. I smiled at my hubby, "Aren't you proud of me?" I asked. Was that a hint of smugness in my voice? Not smart, Lela. Not smart at all.

For some unknown reason, Cecil wasn't smiling. It looked as if he was getting too much sun; his face was flushed beet red, and for whatever the reason, he appeared downright unhappy as he tersely replied, "That's it. I'm done."

"Come on, girls. Let's pack it in," he ordered the girls, "Time to go."

"But Daddy . . ."

"I said, let's go," he said, his voice rising alarmingly.

"But Daddy . . ." Shelly protested bravely.

"Now," he roared in a tone of voice brooking no discussion.

"But Cecil, you haven't caught any fish yet," I said tentatively, wondering why he seemed a little irate. He *was* a volatile alpha male but what could have possibly upset him on this glorious day? "Don't you want to stay a little longer? The fish are biting really well today."

Cecil shot me a lethal look—silent—but deadly. "No," he brusquely retorted. The last kind word—or any word I'd be privileged to hear from him for the rest of the day. Men! I'll never understand them.

On the endless ride home (for me), Shelly spoke up boldly. She had no inhibitions about asking for what she wanted. "That was fun," she said. "Wasn't it, Andi?" Andi was nervously nibbling her fingernails, not sure how to evaluate this experience and afraid to say anything at all. Shelly frequently had to do the talking for her. "Can we do it again next Saturday, Daddy?" Shelly continued fearlessly. "Can we, Daddy? Pleeease?"

"Uhh," he kind of grunted. Was that a "yes" or a "no?" I guess it must have been a "no" since we never—not ever—went fishing together again.

The girls disappeared to the safety of their room to play Barbie dolls as soon as we got home, and I started dinner. Except for Shelly's cheerful chatter, the rest of us ate in silence, the atmosphere as fragile as an eggshell, Cecil checking frequently to make sure Andibeth had one hand in her lap and no elbows on the table. Invariably Andi would forget those cardinal rules, especially when her dad was watching vigilantly, as if he were a hawk ready to swoop down and devour a helpless little songbird.

Immediately after dinner, Cecil disappeared into the living room to watch TV—his normal evening routine. After quietly cleaning up and puttering strategically out of the war zone for a while, I tiptoed upstairs to settle the girls for the night. When Cecil was *really* unhappy, though, he'd turn off the TV—and the lights—lie on the couch and enjoy wallowing to the dulcet tones of Jim Reeves. I groaned inwardly as I heard the melancholy sound of Jim Reeves floating up through the register in the floor, mournfully crooning, "Four Walls . . . cloo-sing in on me." Even on a good day that song would make you want to weep and wail and beat your breast in grief. I knew it was going to be a *very* long night—the kind of night when a privacy fence mysteriously appeared right down the middle of the bed, "No Trespassing" signs liberally posted in big, black, bold print all over it.

While Cecil slept peacefully, I stayed awake a long time, wallowing in my own self-pity, the joy of fishing washed away in a sea of tears. I spent a few minutes pleading with God to intercede on my behalf and soften my hubby's anger. How could he possibly stay mad at a wonderful wife like me? I slipped effortlessly into fantasy land—a comforting place where Cecil finally realized how very much he loved me—and needed me—just as I lay teetering on the brink of death. I recaptured some joy in those few moments—enough to bravely cross the invisible wall and carefully position my generous ice cold butt next to his warm, but totally oblivious, back. He might as well share some of his "heat" in a constructive manner; he needed a little cooling off, anyway.

It would take years of hard work and huge love before he did eventually learn to laugh, and even to laugh at himself. In spite of persevering through the good times—and the bad—and growing closer together as the years have passed, you probably won't be surprised to learn that I'm not a big fan of fishing. Jim Reeves isn't high on my list of favorites, either.

Work, Romance and Genes

I come from a long line of industrious, talented, creative women. The era and place they grew up in necessitated learning certain basic skills just to survive. Skills like sewing and baking and preserving food. My mother started baking bread when she was only fifteen years old. One day, watching her mother struggling to make bread during her mother's mid-life pregnancy, she had offered to take over the task; she never quit baking bread—she was ninety-one years old when she baked her last loaf. But besides normal everyday duties, she also gardened, preserved, canned, quilted, sewed, crocheted, and embroidered. Her apple pie was the best on the planet. The odd thing about it? It wasn't a drudgery for her. None of it. She loved working. She even enjoyed washing dishes! Truly amazing.

My mother was widowed young—just shy of forty-three years old. Although she never re-married, she came close a couple times and periodically found herself attracted to a member of the opposite sex. She yearned for romance—a desire she never lost. When she was eighty-nine, the doctor who hooked up her pacemaker made a big fuss over her. He said that she reminded him of his grandmother. Sometimes a little kindness to a vulnerable, hungry soul can create all sorts of inner turmoil. My mother's love gene immunity had been compromised by long years of romantic loneliness and deprivation, and she proceeded to develop a powerful attraction to her young doctor. I reluctantly, and helplessly, watched her suffer through the throes of unrequited romantic love. I selfishly believed that legitimate romance belonged only to the young and single, but Mother was always "young at heart." I regret to say that I wasn't as gentle or as understanding as I should have been. *Everybody* has a right to love and to be specially loved by another in return; it is the most basic need we have, I think.

In some ways I'm very much my mother's daughter— except—I didn't inherit the "I love to work gene." I'd even go so far as to say, while I disliked much of the repetitive, mundane household chores, I *hated* doing dishes. During my teenage years, prime "dish-washing duty" years, my widowed mother, who only had an eighth grade education had to work in a factory for minimum wage—or less. When our hot water heater failed, she didn't have the financial resources to replace it. That meant we had to heat water on the stove for everything, making even simple tasks more challenging.

On summer vacation, for us kids, that is, my sister and I would wait to start the dishes until right before it was time for Mother to arrive home from work. Occasionally, Mother would get out of work early and we would run in a panic to start the dishes when we saw her little gray Dodge coming down our rural road—not because we feared her, but because we had frittered the day away doing whatever we pleased, while she had been arduously working to earn her small income to pay the bills and feed her family. Clara and I would run wildly through the house to the kitchen, yelling, "Mother's coming. Hurry. Start the dishes." We'd be laughing our heads off— laughing at ourselves for procrastinating, once again, and likely earning a much deserved scolding. A scolding was better than weary silence, though. That weary silence was heavy and intense; besides weighing a ton, you felt as if a dagger were piercing your heart. Mother never lost her high expectations for us, believing that we would naturally do the few simple tasks she left for us just because it was the right thing to do. It's no wonder I still feel guilty forty some odd years later.

It takes some thick-headed people a bit longer than others to learn those challenging life lessons. We seem to like suffering and guilt. We work better under pressure or duress. Put us in a difficult position and our inner gold shines through. Perhaps that's why, even after I was married, I still procrastinated doing the dishes. Although my husband usually kept a regular work schedule, he, too, would occasionally arrive home a little early. You guessed it. There, carefully stacked and waiting, would be the previous night's dinner dishes. Although the house would be in order, I always neatly organized my specific work area before actually addressing the task at hand. I could have done the whole job in less time than I spent preparing to do the job. My husband wasn't quite as easy-going as my mother, though. As much as I hated doing the dishes, he hated seeing them not done. It made him mad. His mad was scary. It vacillated between cutting remarks, passionately delivered—remarks that could instantly flatten you—or—the dreaded silent treatment, which could last a few days and be equally as devastating. When we eventually had a reasonably mature, civil conversation about those dishes, he said to me, "If you really loved me, you'd make sure those dishes were done."

I stared at him in fascination. How was I to know that washing the dishes was a sacred symbol of love? My mother had never told me that. "It has nothing to do with love," I replied defensively. "It's not because I don't love you that I don't wash the dishes; I put off doing the dishes because I *hate* doing dishes." I knew I sounded as if I were whining pathetically.

I was. We reached a tentative peace settlement, obviously a tenuous one. I groveled appropriately—I'm an expert at that craft, and life moved on.

A short time later, feeling somewhat more inclined toward domesticity, (my husband must have been temporarily happy with me) I asked my friend, Sherry, if she would teach me the rudiments of crocheting. I remember how awkward and clumsy my fingers were as she patiently showed me how to hold the crochet hook and yarn. We started with a basic chain. I struggled to master the art of holding the yarn and hook and synchronizing the movements—in and out, up and down—over and over and over again. I finally began to get it. A chain was forming, lop-sided, uneven and long. It grew and grew until it stretched several feet across the room. I silently crowed in pride.

Over the next several weeks, I'd periodically study crochet books, confer with Sherry, and practice, practice, practice. And do the dishes, of course. In spite of my husband's driven nature to work hard, he never seemed to enjoy his labor—it was work—and work was not fun. Nor could he understand my innate propensity for relaxation, especially the desire to lose myself in a book. I loved to read. My two favorite past-times had always been reading and daydreaming. So, if I weren't doing household chores, taking care of our children, or practicing crocheting, I probably had my nose in a book. Although I read a variety of genres: theology, inspirational books, biographies, mysteries and suspense, and an assortment of self-help, how-to books, it was romance novels that I truly loved. I devoured them as if they were candy—chocolate candy, that is—one of my other passions. I could whiz through one of those fluffy books in record time—and still accomplish most of my daily duties. But I far preferred the chocolates and the romance novels to the housework. I don't remember if it was Pollyanna, or Rebecca in the childhood book, *Rebecca of Sunnybrook Farm,* who when asked by her teacher to compose a poem on duty wrote, "When joy and duty clash, duty must go to smash." She got in trouble, of course, and revised her poem to read, "When joy and duty clash, tis' joy must go to smash," or something like that. My hubby hated seeing me read romance novels, too, so I'd often have to quickly hide my novel under another book. Since I wore a perpetual, omnipresent sense of personal imperfection, as if it were a scarlet "A," I likely had a self-help or how-to book going concurrently—something like, "The Art of Understanding Your Husband" or "The Disciplines of a Beautiful Woman." Candy wrappers, the evidence of a closet sweet addict would magically disappear under the pile of tissues I'd accumulated crying over some sad heroine suffering in the throes of unrequited love.

I finally acquired enough skill to begin a crochet project. I started an afghan, one large granny square in various fall colors. Most of one day I maneuvered that hook and thread adding row upon row until I had a square about two feet in diameter. I felt so domesticated and proud. I knew my hubby would be proud, too. When he arrived home from work that day I felt no guilt, (well, maybe just a little), as I sat in my easy chair, emerging afghan carefully displayed on my lap, a visible accomplishment of my day's labor. I imagined how lovely I must look, how inviting, how cozy and comforting to my battle-scarred, tough man who had braved the stressful challenges of the jungle that day. I smiled at him as he walked in, proudly held up my elementary project, and (silly me), asked, "How do you like our afghan?"

He didn't smile. He momentarily studied it. He's a carpenter with a good eye. "It's crooked," he stated bluntly.

I knew he was right—it was blatantly obvious, but being right didn't soften the moment. Exemplary, calm, peace loving Christian that I am, I threw that thing across the room. He wasn't fazed a bit. At some point, I meekly retrieved my work, and eventually completed the afghan. It would grace the back of our sofa for several years, adding a splash of color to the drabness of its surroundings.

I still crochet. I still eat chocolate—very sparingly. I almost always do my dishes immediately after dinner and even enjoy the task. And I still love to read—but—*not* romance novels, not for years and years and years. I learned to enjoy washing dishes and to hate romance novels. I'd rather read true crime. What does that tell you? Here's a hint: I once heard a television host ask the wife of world-renowned Christian evangelist Billy Graham if she'd ever considered divorce over the course of their long marriage. Ruth said, "No," then humorously added, "But I thought about murder a few times."

My mother's work and romance genes stayed healthy till the end—she was almost ninety-two. Mine mutated. It's a good thing my humor gene remains intact.

Assumptions can be Dangerous

"She's just pulling power," I whined to my husband as I adjusted my burgeoning tummy for the night. It was several months prior to my due date in my second pregnancy and I was suffering all the classic symptoms, including a super-sensitive psyche. "I never ask for any special consideration. It isn't fair. Why couldn't she be a little more accommodating?" He turned off the light and patted me gently, not as in comfort, of course, but rather a longsuffering period he was attempting to put on my month long sentence of complaining. As usual, I laid awake a long time, mentally mulling the huge injustice of the situation, and woke up the next morning mournfully singing the same old sad song. I desperately needed to find my inner peace.

We attended a small country church where we were actively involved in several capacities. One of those responsibilities we carried was as leaders of the youth group. Always searching for creative and interesting diversions to keep the youth involved, I asked a friend, who was a hair stylist, if we could make a date for her to instruct the four young female members of the youth group in general hygiene—hair, nails, facials, etc. I thought the girls would enjoy this special treat, devoid of religious instruction. We set a date that worked for both her and me.

I was surprised when I shared that date with my good friend, Carole, the pastor's wife, that she didn't enthusiastically endorse my plans. In fact, she firmly informed me that date was unavailable as *SHE* already had made plans with the girls for that day. I pleaded my case with all the eloquence I could muster, but she remained steadfast and immovable. I began thinking D-I-V-O-R-C-E. Besides possibly leaving the church, a good friendship teetered precariously on the precipice of imminent death. I'm pretty easy going, but this appeared to be a flagrant abuse of authority and inexcusable behavior.

I felt sorry for myself that entire month. I whined. I complained. I nurtured petty, mean-spirited thoughts. I emotionally detached, attending church with a perfunctory attitude, smiling on the outside but inwardly fuming. I'd be present, but I didn't have to like it.

The day of the big betrayal arrived. My desperate husband, weary of listening to my constant whining and complaining, knew he needed to create a diversion. He loaded the large, lumbering Lela, into the car to take me for a nice long ride. I've always enjoyed a leisurely ride over back country roads and it *was* a beautiful day. I started to forget about my grievances. We rode all over the place, and, eventually, past our pastor's house. Pastor Duane was standing outside in his yard and we waved as we drove by. I said to my husband, "Don't you think we should go back? Won't he think that it's odd us being in his neighborhood and not at least stopping to say hello?" He lived about thirty-five minutes away from us.

But my husband seemed disinclined. "Hmmm," he murmured, as if he were pondering a major decision. "Not now. Maybe we'll see if they're home a little later. I thought I saw a riding mower for sale up the road a ways the last time we were in this area. I want to check and see if it's still there."

After driving another twenty minutes—or so—he turned the car around and we headed back. Although Pastor Duane was no longer outside, my husband pulled in the driveway anyway and we strolled to the front door of their home. As I walked in, a choir of smiling ladies greeted me, calling, "SURPRISE!!" Who would have thought? A baby shower—for me—hosted by my good friend, Carole, the pastor's wife, and four young ladies from the youth group.

My stricken conscience wouldn't let me rest. Thankfully, the next day was Sunday and in the moments of congregational praise or petition, I stood to my feet, told my ugly little story and publically asked for Carole's forgiveness, which she graciously granted.

I'm ashamed to confess how many times my errant mind has created difficult situations out of totally innocent circumstances. I would save myself a lot of needless grief and heartache if only I'd diligently work on the "trust" issues and not allow my vulnerable imagination and skeptical mind such free reign. I need to read my Bible more and assimilate the life-enhancing truths into my spirit—truths like Paul's admonition to the church at Philippi . . . "Finally, brothers, whatever is true, whatever is noble, whatever is right, whatever is pure, whatever is lovely, whatever is admirable—if anything is excellent or praiseworthy—think about such things (Phil. 4:8).

The Handle

One crisp, late September morning, the kind of morning that makes you feel energized, invincible and able to take on the world, I decided it was time to move my everyday summer clothes from the convenient armoire, to the more inaccessible closet shelf and replace them with my fall/winter wardrobe, a short journey I make every spring and fall. When I started to unload the tall armoire, I was feeling so motivated that I shrugged off my innate tendency to procrastinate and decided to tackle the broken handle on one of the doors. For several *years,* that handle had been carelessly lying on top of the chest and I would leave the door with the missing handle slightly ajar to facilitate easier access. On this morning, however, I retrieved the handle, studied both it and the door, ascertained the need for a Phillips screwdriver, and went looking in my little cache of household tools that I keep in the bedroom closet. Only flat heads. Did I really want to go *all the way downstairs,* through the family room, the kitchen, the little hallway, and into the cavernous, murky garage, to search through my husband's big, red, sacred tool chest for the right tool? Hmmm . . . well, maybe not today. The armoire had survived just fine for years. I returned the lonesome handle to its resting place on the top of the chest, finished my task and forgot all about that handle.

Then, the phone rang. The news I heard instantly dispelled my sense of peace and well-being. It suggested the potential for an already difficult life situation to become much more complicated. As I often do, I picked up pen and paper and journaled my angst. Not unlike the Psalms in the Bible, my written words are frequently to God, and this was no exception.

I pleaded for divine intervention, basically asking God to "wave" His "magic wand" and make my troubles disappear. I wrote these words, "I can't **handle** one more thing." Even though I had asked for His help, I couldn't let go of my anxiety and fear.

The next day, when I went to open my armoire, I was amazed to see the broken handle attached to the door. I wondered about it, but assumed my husband's capable hands had handled the job.

That evening I thanked my husband for re-attaching the handle to my armoire door. He seemed genuinely puzzled. "What handle?" he asked. I explained the situation and he and I went to view this phenomenon. "I didn't touch it," he replied. "If I happen to notice that the door is ajar as I'm walking past, I just shut it," he said. "But, I didn't fix this handle." He tested it. Pulled on it a bit. Opened and shut it. It was a little loose. "Nope. If I'd repaired it, I'd have done a better job than this."

Various family members offered their theories about this "supernatural" event. My sister thought her recently deceased husband had visited. "It sounds like Dutch," she said tearfully.

My mother was sure my Dad had returned from the other side. "He was always fixing something," she confidently assured me.

Regardless of how the task got done, the difficult situation did not get better. What I had feared most came to pass. The journal entry was brief. . . "The handle on my armoire was miraculously replaced." I got the message, though. Even though I may not always be able to handle difficult life situations, God can. I just need to let Him.

It's a tough one for me, this thing called trust. I may not trust myself, or others, but I want to implicitly trust the Creator of the universe. The Hebrew writer penned these words, "Although he [Jesus] was a son, he learned obedience from what he suffered." Trust—the highest form of love, I think, and its natural consequence, obedience, are irrevocably linked. Situations often aren't resolved the way we think they should be, but an insignificant handle reminded me that a greater intelligence than mine is in control. He will provide the strength and grace needed to navigate successfully when the seas get rough, if only I learn to trust and obey.

The handle, although a bit wobbly, still holds, many years later. My wobbly faith does, too.

"Lord, I believe. Help me overcome my unbelief."

A Good Spanking

When I walked into the Doctor's office for my monthly check-up, several months into my second pregnancy, only one lone lady sat in the waiting room. I didn't know who she was—but she obviously did. From the top of her carefully coiffed hair to the tips of her toes, she was perfectly assembled—not overdone—just right. She looked the way I aspired to look but never quite managed to achieve. As a naturally friendly person, I'm quite comfortable talking to anyone. And, as a book lover, I always notice a fellow reader, and this lady, book in hand, appeared to be someone I might enjoy conversing with. I smiled and said hello when she glanced up from the book that had her mesmerized. Brrrrr. Instantly, a cold north wind blew around that room, the temperature sharply plummeting; icicles formed on furniture and walls. I knew I had inadvertently erred by approaching this hallowed personage. She deigned to return my greeting—barely—with a brief, "Hello." I had never before realized what a powerful message could be conveyed with one little word. You didn't have to tell me twice. I shut my mouth and buried my nose and my wounded ego in my own "no trespassing" accessory—a book.

We sat together in icy silence, wrapped in invisible insulation, choosing not to be contaminated by exposure when another lady bounced in, good humor visibly emanating from her. She smiled inclusively and spoke warm greetings to us. The ice queen almost nodded her head in response. I returned a brief, cool greeting. Why? For one thing this young woman was dressed haphazardly. Her clothes were mismatched, although they appeared to be clean. But, oh—her hair. Her hair looked as if someone had put a bowl on her head and crudely hacked around it—giving her a distinct "Dutch Boy" haircut that stuck out straight at the bottom. Obviously, fashion-consciousness was not high on her list of priorities. I hurriedly raised my book and pretended to be totally absorbed, trying to distance myself.

The doctor's receptionist suddenly called out to me. "Lela," she said, "would you mind changing your next appointment?"

Being the accommodating, good Christian that I am, I said, "Sure. I'm flexible."

"How about Wednesday, in two weeks?" she asked. It was getting close enough to term to warrant more appointments.

"Hmmm, I don't think so," I replied. "I have church that night."

From the other side of the waiting room, the friendly Dutch Boy looked right at me and cheerfully asked, "Prayer meetin'?"

The winds of winter were originating from me, now, as I tersely replied, "No." I was at my intimidating best, brooking no discussion. It wasn't really a lie, although I normally did attend a Wednesday night service called, "prayer meeting." The Wednesday night in question, though, our church was hosting special services for several days—revival meetings—where the lost got saved and the holy got holier. I was way past needing that, of course. I was a spiritually mature, devout follower of Jesus Christ.

I felt a faint twinge inside as the sunshine disappeared behind the cloud that crossed my summery neighbor's face, but I quickly suppressed it. It was more important to me that my wintry neighbor didn't associate me with this unkempt, unpolished lady.

The receptionist and I worked out a viable alternative. Thankfully, the nurse called me back to a room to wait there for the doctor—normally another long wait. Time—time to think—to reflect—to get some perspective. The air in that room had a definite chill, too. I felt it. It seeped deep into my bones, pierced my heart. A still, small voice began to penetrate my arrogance. The voice grew to a thunder and the God of the universe gave me one of the worst "whuppins" of my life. I knew I deserved it. It was not an enjoyable few moments. My inner spirit squirmed in shame. I had judged by exteriors and lost an opportunity to make a friend of someone, undoubtedly, of sterling character—someone who might have enhanced my life with goodness, or, at the very least, brightened a moment in time.

I told God I was sorry, embarrassed and ashamed by my small-minded behavior. I vowed to make amends when I left the office, but, of course, she wasn't there.

It was to be one of the most powerful lessons I ever received as I realized I had treated a good person with the same petty, humiliating treatment I myself had, on occasion, received at the hands of others. What made me so special, anyway? Or my wintry, unfriendly neighbor, for that matter? God doesn't play favorites. In faith we are all equal—race, gender, age, physical appearance, intellect, or socio-economic status do not matter to God. It's a good thing, too, because I have often acted like an immature idiot. But I do have a teachable spirit. My mother always said that whenever I got too cranky or contrary, all I needed to sweeten me up was a good spanking.

Sweet and Savage Snow

Snow is magical, at least when it first arrives, transforming the bleakness of a dormant landscape into a fairy land—a world dressed in pristine bridal finery, promising newness, symbolizing purity. When I was a child, I loved the snow: flopping down in it to make snow angels, sliding downhill, throwing snowballs, catching snowflakes on my tongue, making snowmen, and, when the snow was deep enough, helping carve a labyrinth of tunnels in the front yard. Snow creates a whole new magical playground right in your own yard, and free of charge besides.

Just prior to Christmas one year, we traveled an hour north to visit relatives. Our daughter, Sarah, and granddaughter, Elizabeth went with us. We made a brief stop at my brother Dan's home to drop off a gift. When we pulled into their driveway, Elizabeth, who was a mystical eight-year-old at the time and already appreciative of the beauty in life, exclaimed in awe, "Oh, look at all the clean white snow."

We visited for a few moments before Elizabeth asked permission to go outside and walk in the snow. My brother, Dan and his wife, JoAnne, my hubby, Sarah, and I, all enjoyed watching Elizabeth thoroughly enjoying making footprints in the "clean white snow" before turning our attention elsewhere. When Elizabeth came in she called our attention to the picture window in their living room, which looked out over their front yard. She had carefully and thoughtfully stamped the silhouette of a large heart in the snow. As we drove away, she told us that she had made a smaller heart in front of their basement door in the back. Elizabeth had left behind a visible expression of love. I can't imagine a more constructive use of "clean white snow."

My husband likes certain aspects of snow, too. Although he performs this particular activity less and less frequently as the years go by, he still occasionally performs donuts in empty parking lots, spinning his vehicle in dizzying circles, and he heartily enjoys throwing snowballs with our three grandsons, Sam, Daniel and Matthew. But his favorite snow activity has always been to drive in places "where no man has ever gone before," occasionally causing his cautious wife much anxiety. It's okay if he successfully navigates both in—and out—but, there have been occasions . . . .

Thirty odd years ago, my hubby and I traveled to Scranton to purchase a new black Ford pick-up truck. We had recently bought property and had begun building a little chalet on it. Because of a crust-covered snow, the driveway, a steep incline, was impassable. The framing crew would park at the bottom of the hill and pull tools up on a tarp or cardboard and then slide back down at night. But, we had a new truck and Cecil wanted to "try 'er out," sure he could make it up the drive. As I would often come to experience over the next few years, sometimes, when the weather was bad, you'd have to get a running start. Cecil was/is a good driver, quick thinking with good reflexes, and he already knew that important maneuver. Darkness was falling as we began this adventure. Cecil gunned the black beast and up we went. I was silent—praying, of course. Up. Up. Up. Maybe, just maybe we might conquer this natural adversary. Cecil was feelin' the power. Man. Invincible man. Man against the elements. The kind of challenge that gets the primeval sap running. I could almost hear the savage war cry reverberating through the ages . . . Crazy Horse or Geronimo . . . maybe Tarzan beating his chest. . . "Ahhh-ah-Ahhhhh." Abruptly, the grand adventure came to a screeching halt. We had hit some immovable barrier. Cecil got out to survey the situation.

I was praying fervently, "Please, pleeeease, don't let us be stuck."

"Great. Just great. We're stuck," Cecil informs me in disgust as he crawls back in the cab.

"I'm sorry," I tell him quietly, singing a well-worn refrain, knowing that somehow it has to be my fault that we are in this predicament. He has no idea just how sorry I am.

"Yeah, right. I think I can get her out, though." He put it in reverse and gently backed it up a few inches. He put it in drive. Pulled it ahead a few inches. Back and forth. Back and forth. Gently, tenderly he rocked that truck, like a Mama rockin' a baby. He got out and dug around the tires. He got back in and inched the truck forward, then back, switching gears with ease and speed. But, we were not going anywhere.

I'm silently praying—praying without ceasing, "Please, God, if You care about me at all, please help Cecil get this truck out of this snow bank." You see, I'd had a few prior experiences with some of those "boldly going where no man has ever gone before places," and I remembered how truly awful they had been. When things aren't going well, Cecil gets a little irate. He expects you to read his mind and anticipate what he wants before he even asks; then you must perform the task with speed and expertise. His voice goes down an octave but the volume goes up which is a diplomatic way of saying he yells. He doesn't swear; he just yells—with passion. His yelling is pretty scary.

Even under the masterful hands of my husband, the truck is not moving forward. It appears to be sinking, though. The moment I had feared arrived. "I'm going to get out and push," he says. "You take the wheel." My whole system shut down instantly. I froze. I couldn't think. I couldn't pray. I couldn't even breathe.

"Give it a little gas," he yells to me. I step on the gas. The tires spin enthusiastically. "What are you doing?" he roars belligerently. He goes around to the front of the truck and gets in position, shoulder pressed against the front fender. "Okay. Try it again." I'm scared to death to touch the gas pedal but I give it a tentative push, a feather hit. "What's the matter?" he yells again. "I told you to give it some gas." I give it some gas. Snow flies and the truck settles deeper into its snowy nest. "Move over," he practically spits at me in disgust. "I have to do everything myself." To my horror, a tear trickles down my cheek. I'm feeling very sorry for myself. In fact, I'm having a full-fledged pity party. I don't want him to know that I'm crying but my nose is starting to drip dangerously and I unobtrusively wipe it on my coat sleeve.

He is not so gentle now. He's mad. Mad at the truck. Mad at himself. Mad at me. He furiously rocks the truck back and forth, back and forth, muttering all the while under his breath. Whatever is he saying? Could it be sweet nothings? The words are muffled and garbled, as if he wants me to hear, but doesn't want to be liable for what he's saying. It must be a foreign language. It sounds like "toopid" or "dum bro." Is he talking about the truck or me? Whatever he's murmuring, the obstinate truck doesn't get it; she will not budge. "I'm going to walk down to the neighbor's and call the tow truck," he says in exasperation, finally declaring defeat. He is not a man to give up easily.

The neighbor is an invincible man, too. He wants in on this adventure. He hops in his little jeep and confidently hooks a chain to our new truck. I'm still numb, but thankful my part in this escapade is almost over. Together these two invincible men attempt to free our truck, but they are unsuccessful. I sit alone in the truck—in the dark—while Cecil calls AAA from the neighbor's house. When Cecil comes back, he climbs in the truck and says brusquely, "Triple A is coming. They should be here soon." I don't respond. "I hope you're not pouting," he adds.

Why ever would I be pouting? "No, I'm just being quiet," I reply. It's a tactical statement of survival, not exactly a lie.

We sit in silence. Waiting. The woods are dark and cold around us.

"Do you know what time it is?" Kenny Burdick asks Cecil when he shows up to rescue us. He is not a happy camper. It is 11 p.m. This adventure is several hours old. In just a few brief moments we are back on the road. We drive home in silence.

It was a good long while before we could talk about our late night adventure in the snow bank. Eventually, it got funny, funny enough to laugh about. Nevertheless, the slightest hint of a potential "stuck" situation like that one causes me to immediately freeze up. My heart momentarily stops. I still pray, of course, I just try not to pray with such immaturity— you know the kind of prayer I mean; the desperate "Get me out of here, how can this be happening to me" focus on yourself kind of plea from the depth of your stomach. I am thankful, so very thankful that I haven't had to use my prayers for that kind of rescue in a very long time. And, if we ever get stuck in the snow again, I'm going to get right out and start writing messages in the snow. "Call AAA." It sounds like a plan. Sometimes—often—I'm a coward, though, and prefer to live a peaceful existence. So, instead, I might just stomp hearts all over the place. Maybe he'll be feelin' the love and the savage will become sweet.

Making a Friend
of My Enemy

A lifetime ago, my husband and I moved into a big, old duplex built right into the side of a hill. Painted a jaundiced shade of yellow, almost the color of spicy brown mustard, with brown trim, it perched precariously on a little plateau between the street below and the steep rise behind; a tall stone wall, about twenty steps up and bulging ominously, all that appeared to keep it from sliding into the street below.

Looking out the back window in the kitchen, all you could see was dirt, protruding, twisted gray limbs of trees, scraggly shrubs, and weeds—the decorative cover for earth that went almost straight up. Slightly to the left, a set of broken stone steps, placed there by some craftsman long since gone, meandered up the hill to the garage. The garage faced a short street that ran behind our street, the two streets forming a small triangle, a border for several old homes, ours included. Weathered and ravaged by age and neglect, the garage was not fit for any kind of storage. But the area surrounding it provided an unobtrusive dumpsite for my husband's fledgling construction business. During that first long winter, he accumulated a pile of scrap lumber which we forgot existed once spring rolled around. Out of sight, out of mind. Trouble over that scrap pile loomed on the horizon, however.

A vacant house and garage adjoined our property on the street next to our garage, separated by a small stretch of land. It had been empty for a long time, but early that spring, someone bought it and began some extensive renovations. The scrap pile annoyed Sue, our prospective new neighbor. She called me to complain. I wasn't home. She called again. I promised to speak to my husband. Business was picking up with the good weather, however, and he was never home long enough to address the problem. Sue was not the kind of person to sit back and let life happen. She took action. I had made friends with several of my closest neighbors and one of them confided to me that Sue had been circulating a petition, collecting names, to protest that pile of scrap lumber and force my husband to clean it up.

About that time, someone from the American Cancer Society called and asked me if I would collect donations for their annual fund drive—on my street and the street behind me. I didn't give Sue a second thought when I agreed to do it—not until the night before, that is. I laid awake for several hours contemplating potential scenarios. I needed to find an ethical, responsible solution to my dilemma, that is, to avoid meeting Sue. "I'll just skip her house," I thought. "No, can't do that. Maybe I'll temporarily change my name. Nope, that's not right either." Perhaps, if God weren't too busy, he'd make sure she wasn't home when I stopped by. That was the best case scenario I could come up with but I knew it was not realistic. I needed to be mentally prepared for any eventuality. Then, the answer to my quandary came to me. "I know." I sighed in relief. "I just won't tell her who I am." Resolved, I finally fell asleep.

Bright and early on a beautiful spring day, I set out on this noble mission. I was praying hard as I approached Sue's house, "Oh God, pleeeeease don't let Sue be home." I know God was smiling in anticipation. Sue *was* home. A crew of workmen were there, too. The foreman and Sue were seated on the grass discussing their project as I marched resolutely toward them, heart palpitating thunderously. I smiled bravely at them and brightly said, "Good morning. I'm collecting for the American Cancer Society. Would you like to make a donation?"

Sue smiled warmly up at me from her position at my feet and asked, "What's your name?"

I gulped and said, "I don't think you want to know."

She said, "Oh? Is your name Anderson?" (her last name)

"No." I replied tersely, hoping to get off this dangerous subject. Time momentarily stood still as we stared silently at each other. She was pondering this puzzle and I wasn't about to offer any information about myself.

Suddenly her whole face lit up, illuminated by her epiphany. She jumped to her feet and exclaimed loudly, "You must be Mrs. Buchanan." Without giving me the opportunity to reply, she grabbed my free hand and pulled me, (actually dragged is a better word), down across her yard to the pile of scrap lumber and dramatically announced, "Let me show you my cancer." I listened quietly to her twenty minute dissertation on the grief and heartache she and her family were suffering because of this eyesore. I humbly groveled, apologized profusely and graciously accepted her refusal to donate to the American Cancer Society. She promised to make a contribution "after the mess is cleaned up."

Trembling, but otherwise intact, I hurried home and impressed upon my husband the urgency in dealing with this problem, which thankfully, he promptly did.

Relieved, I tried to forget the whole uncomfortable situation. I planned to avoid Sue in the future. But a few weeks later, Sue called me again. This time, she thanked us for addressing the problem, wondering if I'd like to come up someday and have tea with her. Although it was a nice gesture, this lady seriously intimidated me. But how could I say no to a force like Sue?

A few days later, I found myself seated at her kitchen table in her lovely renovated home. Over the course of the conversation I got to know a bit about Sue. I asked her questions about herself and she seemed happy to share. It seems she was an actress, having played various roles in several soap operas. *"I bet she played the villainess,"* I thought pettily. But performing with her puppets had garnered her more fame as she had even appeared on the "Ed Sullivan" show with them. Currently at work on a novel, some of which she read to me, her primary interest—other than her neighbor's scrap lumber pile, that is—revolved around a local wholeness institute. Although we enjoyed a very nice visit, I sighed in relief as I walked down the hill to the safety of my home.

A year—or so—later, we bought property outside of town and built a little chalet on it, a chalet that resembled a birdhouse perched in the middle of the woods. Sue called me periodically, and I invited her out to visit one day. She loved my cozy home, all done in warm earth tones. A few days later, I received a lovely note in the mail from Sue and a beautiful poem she had written called, "Lela's House." I'm sorry to say the little poem got lost somewhere over the years, but I clearly recall snippets of it. She mentioned the tall oak trees, calling them "silver sentinels lining the driveway," and "high above the Cyclops blinked," a reference to the stars sparkling in the night sky. But the last line touched me deeply . . . "then, from your house, His voice."

My whole relationship with Sue could have easily been one of acrimonious hostility. I felt inferior, intimidated and severely disadvantaged at various times with her. I had to work hard to do what I knew was right; I'm glad I did. When she looked at me, she apparently saw a glimmer, a slim resemblance to the Creator.

I lost touch with Sue after we moved to Stroudsburg. I heard from various sources that she stirred the pot many times over various issues through the years. Sometimes life requires a good pot stirrer. Once again, however, I can clearly see, in retrospect, that God wanted me to become better than I was through this experience. He didn't want me to take the easy way out. Even though I inwardly "kicked and screamed" initially, I learned another vital life/God lesson. And I turned a potential enemy into a friend.

Too Puffed Up

I've learned a lot of life lessons the hard way. Someone warning you of potential pitfalls and heartaches just doesn't carry the same clout as a two-by-four along-side the head. Of course, if you live long enough and are fortunate enough to have children, there is no danger of becoming too proud—they'll make sure of that! A husband might help keep you humble, too. My life has been so full of humbling experiences, it's a wonder I even appear in public. I read an account of Ben Franklin's take on the virtue of humility that went something like this: He prayed fervently for the virtue of humility, but every time he felt that he was close to acquiring it, he got proud.

It's difficult to have an accurate picture of oneself. If the only mirror we ever choose to look in gives us exclusively positive reviews, (or negative) we're going to develop an unhealthy self-image. Notice I said, "Choose." Not only do we tend toward *self* blindness, we often see what we choose to see in others. It's easier that way. We don't have to deal with the ugly stuff then—in ourselves or others. I call that deconstructive love as it reinforces negative actions and attitudes, diminishing rather than enhancing the character of a person.

We've all experienced those awkward moments in life, moments when we smile and wave at someone who we think is waving and smiling at us only to realize it's an exchange with someone behind us. I actually remember a time when I was probably eight or nine years old, grabbing hold of a ladies dark blue coat at church and tugging on it, thinking it was my mother. A very kind lady—Leah, I later learned—looked down at me in surprise. I gazed back at her, equally surprised, let go of her coat as if it were a hot potato and said, "Oh, you're not my mother." Young as I was I still remember the sudden rush of embarrassment at that harmless mistake.

My sister, Clara, wanted Mother, too. When she was twelve or thirteen she mistakenly greeted her very male music teacher one day by calling, "Mommy," as she walked in the music room. Since he saw himself as an accomplished Casanova, and was a known philanderer, he wasn't too pleased with her identity confusion.

One day my husband needed to meet an old codger who worked for his excavator at a gas station on Route 402. I rode along with him that day. Cecil rolled down his window and the guy leaned in to talk with him. "What 'er we gonna do with this here pretty young girl?" he asked.

The only girl I saw was me, and feeling confused—since I'd never met the man, but, very flattered, I laughed and replied, "Thank you, but I'm not that young."

He didn't even look at me; he totally ignored me as if I didn't even exist. I rapidly found out why. He gestured behind him and continued, "She don't have no place ta go," and proceeded to tell my husband about the plight of a young lady standing over by the phone booth at the edge of the asphalt. We ended up taking the young lady home with us, feeding her, letting her spend the night, giving her a few bucks and buying her a bus ticket home to California. She was a very pretty, young, lost soul. Her predicament was solved, but my inner "face" stayed red a long time. I wonder what *he* was thinking?

Only one time did my girls and I ever take a vacation together without my husband. Traveling to the Bahamas leaving Newark via Miami, I needed to use the bathroom. I'd flown a few times but rarely used the facilities. I wasn't sure if I had the door properly latched but I desperately had to pee. Imagine my chagrin—just as I began standing up, pants around my knees, to come face-to-face with an equally surprised gentleman, opening the door expecting an unoccupied restroom. "I'm sorry," he mumbled, red-faced and flustered, and hurriedly shut the door.

Why do we always use this totally inane phrase? "That's okay," I'd replied. It wasn't, of course. I went back to my seat praying that I would never see the man again. We had a layover in Miami. What are the chances? I only saw the guy about three more times. I'm a blusher, too, but I think he had me beat.

As embarrassing as those kinds of experiences can be, however, there is not much of a lesson in them. Sometimes humility is earned by default. The year I was fifteen I attended a church youth camp for a week—the summer of 1965. Although a Holiness camp meeting had been an integral part of my summer all my growing up years, youth camp was vastly different. For one thing, the stringent dress rules were relaxed—jeans were acceptable apparel. The primary message was the same, though—calling wayward souls to the straight and narrow path. When you're fifteen, however, the world still revolves around you and the fulfillment of your physical and emotional needs, and you carelessly relegate that liability to others. Personal responsibility is not a familiar concept at that stage of your emotional development.

Besides the relaxed dress code and activities geared to our age group, instead of cabins, we slept in tents—girls on one side of the hillside, boys on the other. Each tent held about ten little army cots and was ruled by a camp counselor. The year I attended, my counselor was a lovely, mature lady named Alice who I absolutely adored. She loved me, too.

Besides overseeing the girls in her tent, Alice was also responsible for coordinating the camp work schedule. She made up a chart of duties: duties like washing or drying dishes for every meal, sweeping the floors of the chapel or dining hall, cleaning the bathrooms, etc. We were all expected to do our part but with such a large work pool to draw from, duties were assigned sparingly. For most of us, doing dishes with a girlfriend and a couple of cute guys was actually pretty stimulating work. Still, there were always a few difficult attendees who resisted any kind of task—and they didn't mind expressing their distaste. Not righteous me, of course. Alice's job wasn't easy, especially since she had such a tender heart and unassuming demeanor.

Alice and I had quickly developed a warm rapport. I guess that's why she felt comfortable asking me if I'd mind this assignment. "Would you clean the toilets on Thursday, for me, Lela?" she asked one day, chart in one hand, pencil in the other.

I glibly and thoughtlessly replied, "Ewwww. Toilets?" My face matched my voice, both dripping with distaste. My mouth reluctantly said, "Okay." My tone of voice and facial expressions screamed, "No way."

Every day I checked the daily posted chart for my duties. Washing dishes. Drying dishes. The week passed. Never—not once did my name appear with bathroom duty. Alice never gave me a toilet to clean all week long. By the end of the week, my conscience was seriously smitten. I knew I had disappointed my beloved counselor. Without saying one word, Alice had taught me a powerful lesson. I may not have cleaned a dirty toilet that week, but my dishonorable behavior shamed me so deeply, that my dirty conscience got a much needed spritz. Unfortunately, my inner person still had some built-up residue clinging tenaciously to me that would require repeated scrubbing with a stiff bristled brush to eradicate. God wasn't in a hurry, though. The process to "become" is a costly life-long journey. Whether or not I enjoyed all of the process, I innately understood, even then, that it was worth the effort.

My life has been filled with humbling moments, but I'm going to share just one more. Mid-to late-forties are hard years for women as our reproductive systems begin to rebel. Changes occur in our bodies, minds and emotions signaling both an ending and a beginning. We call it menopause; the generation before us called it, "The Change." Whatever you call it, a transition takes place—often painful, usually uncomfortable. We struggle to once again define ourselves. I've read that the indigenous "first peoples" believed that a woman is just truly beginning to come into her own at this time in her life. She should know who she is and should not be plagued by the miscellaneous insecurities or longings that may have haunted her in younger years. I like that mindset. We may not be "spring chickens" any more but we are not ready to be put on the back burner, either. As my eldest sister Jennie once spiritedly said to me, "Speak for yourself" when I alluded to us as "a pair of old hens." She qualified herself as a "summer hen," a softer, gentler perspective on aging than what I had so bluntly uttered.

Anyway, I did find a greater sense of purpose in those transitional years as I began studying for the ministry. Actively involved in my church, I held a diverse array of positions. Not only did I serve on the LBA (local board of administration), the highest governing body in the local congregation, I also served as the VC (Vice chairman), the highest lay position in the church—for one year.

The church was going through a change, too, and we had interviewed several pastoral candidates before hiring a charismatic young man. We all fell in love with Pastor Dennis and I felt honored to be serving under him as vice chairman of the board.

One day, about two months into Pastor Dennis' term, he called me from his office at the church to discuss some item of business. I love to talk theology and once the business was settled, we moved effortlessly into a stimulating theological discussion. I had the floor—or, maybe a more apt term might be—the soapbox. I was on it and passionately pontificating some profound point. When I paused for a breath, he said, "Wow!"

"This is really good," I thought to myself. "A good beginning." A young pastor should be impressed with the Godly leadership of his board—specifically me, of course.

Before I could continue, however, he added, "I just saw a tree fall." From his vantage point in his second floor front office, he could view both the side and the front of the area around the church. While he'd been listening to me go on and on, making appropriate affirming noises, "Mmmm—hmmm," or "yes," he'd also been avidly watching a tree cutter at work.

I laughed to myself, wound the conversation up, and wisely recognized the significance of the moment. Sometimes you can get too puffed up—even doing the Lord's work. I enjoyed a good laugh and my proud ego received a much needed adjustment.

Life is filled with teachable moments, often accompanied by heartache and tears. The Psalmist tells us that God stores our tears in a bottle. That's a good place for them. It comforts me to know that God is with me in my dark moments. I am equally as pleased, however, to imagine the Creator of the Universe laughing with me, also sharing the light-hearted or embarrassing moments with me. "Laugh with your friends . . . share tears," paraphrases Eugene Peterson in *The Message*. When there is no one else, God is a wonderfully safe place, always present to share the moment with us.

Jacob and Esau

We always had pets as we were growing up, primarily cats and dogs, but occasionally a squirrel, raccoon or chipmunk briefly appeared in the picture. I never recall being afraid of the animals, or particularly committed to them, either. They lived along side of us companionably, as a part of the family, yet separate and distinct from us. We loved our pets but didn't hover over them or nurture them as many people do. I guess ambivalence best describes our attitude toward most of the critters in our young world—with a few notable exceptions: a pet red squirrel named Frisky; a black Labrador retriever called Mitzi; and Whiskers, a white tomcat. And that ambivalence continued into adulthood—until Jacob and Esau became part of the family.

Esau was a gray and white tomcat who we adopted as a kitten. I've always liked cats—most everything about them: their fiercely independent nature, their natural cleanliness, the ease in potty training, their playfulness, and the comfort they add to a home, curled up napping in a warm sunny spot. What I don't like about cats, besides fur that sheds copiously, and an obsession with butt washing, is watching them torment and torture chipmunks and other small creatures before devouring them. Nevertheless, Esau, named after the biblical half of the famous brothers (Jacob and Esau) because he seemed unusually "hairy," was a delightful cat with a pleasant personality. When the kids were off to school and my husband gone to work, Esau would follow me around as I did my household chores. When I worked in the kitchen, he laid on the rug close by. He dutifully followed me up the stairs and found a comfy spot to rest while I made the bed and dusted the floors. The girls loved him, too, and he tolerated many of the various capricious whims they inflicted on him.

Esau was an indoor-outdoor cat, that is, he freely came and went as he chose. Early every spring, he'd disappear for days. My mother said he was out prowling for willing females. I'd begin to fret, worrying that he was hurt or dead. Eventually, he'd nonchalantly stroll back home as if he'd never been gone, expecting to be treated like royalty. I'd scold him for being out chasing women while I'm home anxiously pacing the floor over him. I'd often sing to him, "Don't come home a drinkin', with lovin' on your mind." His ears would flatten in exasperation, and possibly pain, and he'd wander off looking for a friendlier welcome.

One traumatic day, Esau came home from an outside jaunt, dragging his hind legs, a malady that rapidly worsened. The veterinarian wasn't sure whether Esau had been hit by a car or if he had some kind of terminal illness. Andrea and Sarah hovered over Esau, even manually expressing his bladder as the vet had taught them to do. His intelligent, bright green eyes surveyed his kingdom from restricted quarters, that is, he could move but it was arduous work, dragging his rear legs across the floor. Even with the back half of his body now paralyzed, you could see in his eyes that the fierce mighty warrior still lived inside this handicapped body.

We had reservations to fly south to spend Christmas vacation at our home in Florida and we reluctantly boarded Esau with our veterinarian. Andrea, who was driving now, signed the consent form giving the vet permission to euthanize our beloved pet, should he feel Esau's condition warranted it. However, our hopes were still high that Esau would recover under the doctor's vigilant care.

It was late when we arrived home and we quickly perused the accumulated mail on the kitchen counter, collected for us by our friend, Bill. Andrea opened a card addressed to her—a sympathy card expressing the condolences of the veterinarian and his staff on the death of our pet. We all stood there in shock—shock that rapidly turned to grief and we hugged each other and wept. We loved our cat, and we would never again find one who would become such an integral part of our family.

Part way through Esau's reign (cats innately understand that they are king or queen of their domain), we also acquired the other half of the brother team—a dog we named Jacob. If you remember the Bible story, Jacob was a schemer from the get-go. He stole his brother, Esau's, birthright and his blessing, then ran far away to his Uncle Laban's house. It took a lot of hard knocks before Jacob finally grew up. During the process, though, he continued to live up to his reputation—scheming and deceiving for his own profit and gain. Like throwing the cat out the window, Jacob always managed to land on his feet, somehow.

Our dog Jacob would have made the biblical Jacob proud. His primary vice, one in which he especially excelled was thievery. Soccer balls, baseballs, footballs, baseball mitts and other miscellaneous items would periodically and mysteriously appear in our yard. Since we live in a rural area, we were never sure where these items came from. The thing about it—Jacob was the best-natured mutt I've ever known. He could charm the socks off you, and he cheerfully endured our youngest daughter, Sarah, playing "dress-up" with him. Besides dressing him in various clothing items, she'd drape all kinds of necklaces around his neck and he'd smile disarmingly for the camera. He had an intense zest for life and he loved passionately and indiscriminately. Oh yes, and he *loved* to steal. He'd come home from a short jaunt totally exhausted, flop down at your feet and smile up at you with joy. You knew he'd been up to no good, but how could you be mad at such an adorable rascal?

My mother lived in an apartment attached to the rear of our home. Because she was diabetic, and in danger of developing nasty foot ulcers, her doctor sent her to a podiatrist for regular treatments to her feet—basically, she was getting professional pedicures. Dr. Wilson was about my age, nice looking and personable, although a bit of a snob—and—this is critical information, my closest neighbor. A small cluster of trees and an abandoned garage separated our houses. You couldn't actually see his home, except in the winter, and then only minimally through the many trees.

One day I stepped outside to call Jacob, only to see him come bounding enthusiastically through those very trees, a baseball mitt clenched in his teeth. He was grinning widely, drooling heartily, his tail wagging with gusto as he collapsed at my feet, gently laying his precious contraband down in front of me—a love offering. Now wasn't that sweet?

All the pieces immediately fell into place as the scales dropped off my eyes with a thud—a thud I felt in the pit of my stomach. I'm just too ethical to ignore such egregious behavior. I knew I'd have to make it right but I wasn't looking forward to humbling myself to my pompous neighbor—a neighbor I'd be seeing soon as my mother had her monthly appointment in a few days.

I cleaned the mitt up, polished my little speech and marched bravely into battle. "Hello, Dr. Wilson," I began. "Ummm. Uhhh. I have a confession to make." I pulled the mitt out of the bag and handed it to the doctor. "I'm sorry to admit this but I'm pretty sure my dog stole this from your yard. He's a thief but he's a good-natured, friendly thief." I'm smiling, nervously stumbling over my words, trying to be funny. The doctor is not smiling.

"We accused our son of carelessness for losing this mitt and insisted he'd have to buy a new one out of his allowance," he told my mother and me in a frosty, condescending tone of voice. I could feel myself shriveling into my lowly worm demeanor. Unfortunately, I wasn't done confessing.

"I'm so sorry about this. Please tell your son how much I regret his inconvenience. I'm afraid to tell you that my marauding canine has sniffed out a few other items. There is a battered soccer ball and a seriously wounded football in my yard, too. I think they might have belonged to your boys. That dog is such a character." Dr. Wilson's face did not look friendly. I reached in my pocket and pulled out a fifty dollar bill. "I'd like to make restitution. I don't know how much those items cost but please accept this toward a new ball," I said, groveling now in humiliation.

He didn't hesitate to take the money. And it was very obvious he'd like to see both me and my dog moldering in a human doghouse with bars and locks. As my mother and I left his office, we decided right then and there to find a new podiatrist. It wasn't that we didn't like Dr. Wilson, but he had denied me a gracious response to my genuine attempt at an honorable resolution. We had hoped for a kinder reaction.

When both Jacob and Esau were gone from our lives, I vowed not to let myself get attached to a pet again. It's like having a couple more kids in the family—more pleasure, but more problems, too. However, over the years two more cats would choose us for family and "Pirate" makes his home with us at the present. He's a nice cat, and a good hunter. But although he's lived here for probably seven years, and I am always kind to him, I have remained emotionally distant. Ironically, my husband, who never liked cats, has bonded with him, though.

I bravely faced my dog's innocent victim and confessed Jacob's sins—knowing I was ultimately culpable for his crimes. Was I brave enough to share the story with my type A personality husband who would have been appalled at my ownership of this crime and angry that I felt the need to make restitution? Hmmm. Maybe not. So, my dear, darling, husband—Cecil—now you know the rest of the story. The guilt is gone—relief—confession *is* good for the soul! I wonder . . . should I tell him about the time I . . . hmmm . . . maybe later.

A Blessing in Dust

On the first day of spring in 1993, while cleaning house, I paused in the main foyer at the base of the stairs and noticed that the old-fashioned hall tree had a visible layer of dust on it. I collect angels, and on the base of this piece of furniture I had positioned three of them: a tall (about 1 ½ foot') natural wooden one held the center spot, flanked on either side by musical revolving angels of lesser stature. I got on my hands and knees, removed the angels and sat them on the floor next to me. With dust cloth in hand, I was about to remove the vestiges of several weeks of accumulated dust when I noticed an unexpected imprint in the dust. The angel on the left had left no visible sign. The tall angel in the middle left a clearly defined X and the angel on the right, a bold O.

As is often my habit, I carry on mental conversations with God as I'm doing my housework, seeking wisdom to deal responsibly with life's many challenges, expressing doubts or fears to a safe place, and/or interceding for the needs of others. Since much of life is fraught with strife and tension, grief and pain, I often whine and complain to the Lord, too. I'm not trying to make light of life's burdens. But as difficult as they may be, they are usually the catalyst driving our spirits into a deeper relationship with our Creator. This particular day, I had been totally absorbed in an ongoing dialogue about a particularly challenging situation. . . "Why, Lord? Why is it so hard? What should I do, Lord?"

Although it may sound fanciful, it was at that very moment in our dialogue, that I noticed the often overlooked piece of furniture, decided to dust it and received a message from God. It was to be a response I would eventually learn to recognize as His normal response. My selfish prayers—those, "Help me" petitions for deliverance from various situations and problems— would be answered by a wiser intellect than mine—not by ironing out the wrinkles for me—not by magically transporting me to a better place. How did He reply? He gave me a holy/heavenly kiss and hug to assure me that He cared, then sent me on my way, giving me the privilege of figuring it out on my own. I've often said that it seems I have to learn every life/God lesson the hard way.

Somewhere through the years of challenges of everyday life, I realized that God appears to care more about my reactions to the various life situations I'm confronted with, than the situations themselves. That is, He doesn't magically make hard things disappear, knowing that if I persevere, I will stretch my heart and mind and spirit to achieve more, to become better, to grow wiser, and, hopefully, more merciful and compassionate by working through those challenges. He makes "it better" but not easier, just as any wise parent would do.

Testimonies

Although I try to be sensitive to the intrinsic need for validation of those around me and express my gratitude to them for who they are as a person, or what they're doing right, I'm a little uncomfortable listening to accolades and tributes being heaped upon a celebrity or an honored person. It doesn't feel authentic to me. I think there are better ways to show appreciation for someone's successes or accomplishments.

It's a little like one of those rare occasions when my hubby decides to pay me a compliment; "Hey, Beautiful," he gushed one morning as I stumbled past him sleepily, hair flying in all four directions, worn jammies drooping wearily. You know—absolutely—positively—for sure—that is serious kissing up for some ulterior motive. Or why can't he tell me my hair looks nice after a fresh haircut, instead of observing as on one such recent occasion after a thorough perusal of my newly coiffed person, "Nice shirt." And how about the time we were watching a TV talk show together, and a svelte, meticulously stylish Olivia Newton-John, dressed in spandex and high heels walked across the screen and my hubby looked pointedly at size fourteen, lumpy, frumpy old me—then, pointedly at her, and with a wicked gleam in his eye innocently remarked, "She's about your age, isn't she?" It's no wonder I look suspiciously at anyone offering me a tidbit of praise. I invariably think they're merely mouthing meaningless and/or insincere platitudes, or, in plain English, BS (not what you're thinking, either—BS stands for baloney sandwiches, of course).

We all worship something or someone. I have a friend who takes offense at the idea of a Creator who needs to be worshiped. I suppose you could argue that does seem egotistical, unless you analyze our innate propensity to "worship" a god of our own choice or making, e.g., money, fame, intellect, knowledge, strength, beauty, etc. Since I believe in God as the creator, sustainer, redeemer of life, I don't have a problem attributing the goodness in my world to him. My heart's desire is to know him and I'm thankful that he has drawn me to himself with irresistible grace. My faith defines me and supplies me with both a reason to live and a reason to die; God deserves to receive my praise. All that, however, doesn't necessarily mean I'm always fast on my feet to offer a testimony.

I was privileged to see—first-hand—real fervor, passion and zeal for the Lord during my formative years. Because of my mother's affiliation with a "Holiness" church, I had the opportunity to observe many followers of Jesus Christ expressing their devotion to their savior. One of the most visible opportunities for congregational participation involved giving a testimony, that is, you stood up and shared how God had transformed your former state of degradation to one of piety. I enjoyed hearing many of those testimonies as they were stirring glimpses of lives changed through the grace of God. I listened intently, and can still recall a few specific illustrations that made an impact on my young life. But, I didn't speak; I sat silently.

Of course, I did eventually open my mouth, initially because, basically, I had no choice. My sister, Ellen, who is eight years older than me, taught the young girls' Sunday school class at camp meeting one year. I usually skipped Sunday school at camp meeting since the evangelistic service that followed would provide me with abundant spiritual nourishment, but when your big sister is in charge, you step lively to your appointments. Ellen offered her small class of young girls the privilege of voluntarily sharing their faith. Cheerfully chattering away, we all instantly shut-down, morphing into mutes. Our little corner of the cavernous tabernacle became a silent, solemn sanctuary. Most teachers encourage class participation—it demonstrates attentiveness. Ellen wasn't about to let the moment pass into oblivion, willing to wield her considerable clout as teacher, elder (she was likely between eighteen and twenty years old—almost an antique) and, of course, older sibling—a born boss in familial hierarchy. "Lela," she said, fixing a stern eye on me, "Would you like to share what Jesus has done for you?" Although it vaguely resembled a request, I knew it to be a non-negotiable command.

At that stage of my life, my widowed mother, a devout follower of Jesus, fulfilled my needs for food, shelter, and love. God might have been the ultimate source, but he was "once-removed" as if he were distantly related. My real faith rested firmly in my mother, although I was not astute enough to consciously apprehend that truth. With Ellen's eyes intently willing me to speak, however, I had to say something, even though I didn't really have anything to say. My knowledge of God was vicarious knowledge—gleaned from what the faithful said and/or did at church and from my mother's active faith. It was to be my first testimony, but I have long since forgotten whatever I fearfully mumbled. I only remember feeling afraid. Not of Ellen (well, maybe just a little afraid), except, of course, I knew she loved me. My real fear was of making a fool of myself, of exposing my inadequacy to the other girls and risking ridicule.

A year or so later and all of thirteen or fourteen years old, I was spending a week with Ellen and her husband, Bob. They lived in a lovely apartment in a pretty residential section of a small village—several houses up from the modest "Holiness" church they attended regularly. That Sunday, the guest pastor invited anyone who wished, to join him for a "class meeting" he would be facilitating immediately following the worship service. There was only one attractive young man in the service that morning, and I deliberately dallied to see if he would stay with his mother. He did. That made it a mandatory meeting for me even though I had no clue what a class meeting might possibly be. So, I stayed behind when Bob and Ellen left for home. About a dozen people stayed, too, scattered sparsely about the sanctuary.

I sat silently waiting for the meeting to start, my mind already rushing into romance with the unknown young man. Almost to the altar to join our hearts together in Holy Matrimony, my delightful reverie was interrupted by the speaker opening the meeting with prayer. As heads bowed in reverence, I snuck a quick peek at my future husband just in time to see him slip quietly out the door! Not the way my fantasy was supposed to unfold. Sitting near the front, I was stuck, and it rapidly became apparent that I had made a serious error in choice. One by one the believers stood up to share their testimonies, i.e., what Jesus had done or was currently doing in their lives. I remember thinking to myself, "They won't expect me to speak; I'm young, and a visitor besides." I began some serious negotiations with God—fervently pleading for divine intervention—a maneuver

I'd attempt frequently in the years ahead. The queue of waiting participants kept shrinking until—horror—of—horrors—only I remained. My leg was swinging furiously, my heart palpitating thunderously. Numb with fright, I gazed helplessly at the pastor, an anxious plea in my eyes. He radiated benevolence as he smiled at me kindly, expectantly—but without mercy—waiting patiently for that one final testimony. My second opportunity to express my devotion to Jesus and, once again, I have no idea what meaningless, inane words issued from my mouth. They must have been acceptable, though, because no one laughed or shunned me as the meeting closed. My knees were shaking as I hurried to the safety of my sister's home. Class meeting? It might have worked for John Wesley, but besides having to testify against my will, I'd just lost my future husband. How pathetic is that? I planned to cross class meetings off my social calendar—forever!

Many years later, having grown in both confidence and spiritual maturity, I often stood to share my testimony. Even though I still felt a bit anxious, I rarely struggled to find words to express my love for God . . . until . . . . For several years we had been attending a church we dearly loved. Unaware of any major problems, we were surprised to learn of some serious negative undercurrents—the source, I was personally to experience, came from one woman in a high position. One day she called me on the telephone and unexpectedly subjected me to one of the most vicious tirades I have ever experienced, maliciously maligning various ladies of the church—ladies I knew and loved. Nor did she exclude me from her list of sinners. I didn't yet know—much to the credit of the other ladies in the church who had suffered silently, that she indiscriminately attacked us all—we all eventually made her infamous list.

Anyway, shortly after the unsettling phone call, I went to church for the Wednesday evening prayer meeting/Bible study in fear and trepidation. Skulking cautiously, as if I were on a covert mission, I sidled in between my mother and my hubby, planted my butt firmly in the pew, and flanked on either side by my protective shield, prepared to remain invisible until the service was over. The chorus of an old hymn ran repeatedly through my mind, "I shall not be, I shall not be moved. I shall not be, I shall not be moved. Just like a tree, that's planted by the water, I shall not be moved." Yeah, right.

The associate pastor was in charge on this night and after an opening prayer, announcements and a few hymns, Dan decided to open the floor for testimonies. Since this was a purely voluntary exercise, I didn't need to worry about participating; I could remain an unobtrusive presence, sit silently through the service, and escape to the safe haven of home in a few short minutes. Sister Chatfield, a dear old saint who always sat in the second pew from the front, immediately stood to her feet, ready to express her love for the Lord. Inexplicably, however, as she finished her little testimony she wistfully asked Dan if we could do testimonies "like we used to do sometimes"—that is, when someone finishes his or her testimony they can call on someone else they'd like to hear from. Dan liked her suggestion and readily agreed. Sister Chatfield turned around, beaming happily from ear to ear and said, "I'd like to hear from Sister Buchanan"—me, in other words. (At that time, all believers were addressed as Brother or Sister—a sign of respect and affection.)

I gulped in shock, slid to my feet as if pulled by some invisible yet irresistible force and said, "I love the Lord and

I know He loves me," and slid back down into the pew—a seamless, surreal, economic moment in time.

I'm an extrovert by nature, and although Dan and his lovely wife, Janie, were good friends of ours, they were unaware of my newly acquired reticence. Dan felt totally comfortable lightheartedly ad-libbing, "I don't think she's done. Did she sound done to you?" he cheerfully asked the congregation. Instantly the focus of many sets of smiling eyes, I was once again helplessly propelled to my feet. I don't remember what I added—I only know that I successfully maneuvered through the service and arrived safely—intact—at home. I had survived another one of those awkward life moments that only becomes hilarious in retrospect.

"Always be prepared to give an answer to everyone who asks you to give the reason for the hope you have . . . with gentleness and respect," the apostle Peter wrote in his first epistle. If that's part of the criteria for being a follower of Jesus, I know that I've often failed—but, I'm sure God has enjoyed a few hearty laughs watching the comedy scenes of my life. I just wish there weren't so many of them.

Words are often inadequate to communicate our understanding of God and I am not hesitant to admit that I've struggled with many questions and doubts about that sacred invisible reality much of my life. Yet, I know with certainty that I could not sail through the tumultuous sea of life without faith in a loving navigator or hope that I would safely reach the other shore. So, although I try to avoid proselytizing, I rarely pass on those serendipitous opportunities to share my faith wherever and with whomever I may find myself. My heart's desire, though, is to model Christ-likeness so effectively that my life speaks volumes of praise and affirmation to the Creator without me uttering a word aloud. I strive wholeheartedly to be an authentic, genuine, living testimony of God's amazing grace and tremendous love.

Claustrophobia

The only occasion in my life when I actually went on a "business" trip with my husband, we traveled all the way from the northeastern most corner of Pennsylvania across the country to the city of San Francisco. Cecil, his business partner, Jack, and their sales manager, Ed, were attending a three day seminar for a *Better Homes & Gardens* real estate franchise they owned at the time. Marie, Diane and I, the three wives were included in the package. That is, the seminar included a schedule for the spouses, too. We all stayed at the elegant Westin St. Francis, a beautiful hotel in the heart of downtown San Francisco.

While the men attended workshops and training sessions, not necessarily intellectually stimulating, we ladies enjoyed miscellaneous fun activities, including a bus tour of the city. I most especially remember admiring *The Painted Ladies*, a row of impeccably maintained Victorian homes. By the third day, the gentlemen began to feel deprived, listening to us regale them with the highlights of our days and they decided to play "hookie" on our final full day—a skill I suspect they were all accomplished pros at executing.

After breakfast the next morning, the six of us made our way to Fisherman's Wharf. We took the tourist boat ride out to see Alcatraz Island. We meandered slowly up the "Strip," periodically stopping to check out a shop or tourist attraction like *Ripley's Believe it or Not*. Cecil wanted to venture into a storefront claiming to be *The Haunted Gold Mine* and we all tagged along. We wandered through darkened hallways with various spectral displays—fake skeletons, for instance, with ghostly noises permeating the air. It was definitely not a polished museum, a fact we had all agreed upon as we laughingly stepped into a rickety, wooden elevator to begin our descent into the depths of the haunted mine, the grand finale of this little tour. Abruptly, the elevator lurched to a stop. We waited briefly for the door to open. It didn't. Did I mention I'm seriously claustrophobic?

For instance, while prepping for dinner once upon a time, I went into our pantry to retrieve some ingredient only to have the light instantly go out—the switch is outside the door—and the door slam shut. The guilty party? My mischievous daughter, Sarah. Since she was slight of build I might have been able to push the door open, except she effortlessly recruited her older sister, Andrea, and together—in complete synchronicity, for once—they held that door firmly shut. I'm normally pretty unflappable. Not this time. I freaked out. Smoke was billowing out of every bodily orifice I own. "You girls let me out of here, right this minute. I mean it," I'm yelling frantically. "This is not funny, girls. You're in big trouble," I threaten menacingly. Trouble? Yeah, right. Somebody thinks it's funny. I can hear stifled laughter out there. They released their captive and faced the music totally unfazed by my extreme reaction. In fact, they looked downright pleased with themselves, demonstrating not a bit of remorse for having subjected their poor old mother to such trauma. I probably needed counseling after such Mom abuse, but instead used it as story material—a kind of therapy, I guess. (I was amused myself, in retrospect. Don't tell them, though. I'd hate to suffer through a repeat performance. I'm getting too old.)

Anyway, here we were—six of us—confined in a little gray wooden box—buried alive. In a matter of seconds we began to demonstrate our natural dispositions, and it wasn't pretty. Cecil and Jack, both alpha males, are yelling orders at the top of their lungs. "Hey, let us out of here. We're stuck." There is no response. "Are you deaf? Open this door. Right now. We're stuck in here." They're pounding on the walls, frustrated by their impotence in this situation. They're both used to speaking, then watching people scurry to fulfill their every command. "You'll hear from our lawyer," they threaten. But there is nobody listening out there. And since this is pre-cell phone technology, we cannot communicate with the outside world. They are not deterred, however, but continue a verbal barrage of orders and threats.

Marie is mad as a hornet, too. And claustrophobic. She adds a few colorful phrases to the mix. She is crying—and swearing heartily—and yelling furiously.

Diane is practically comatose. She has collapsed on the floor. She's claustrophobic, too. She's crying, telling the deaf around her that she's claustrophobic. "Don't you understand that I can't handle this?" she asks plaintively, obviously a victim of some capricious whim of fate directed specifically at her. She murmurs continuously about her sad predicament.

Diane's husband, Ed, as employee to Cecil and Jack, must defer to their leadership. It's their problem to get us out of this underground vault. He's the court jester. He waits for his moment—the moment when others have paused from their ineffective attempts at being rescued. He holds out his arms, dangling his hands and wiggling his fingers. "We can eat me first," he says humorously. Nobody laughs. Except Ed.

What about me? I'm also claustrophobic. I stood in the corner, watching this amazing fiasco in fascination, momentarily distracted from my own anxiety. As I looked around our prison I happened to see a tiny glimmer of light in the corner of the ceiling of this decrepit wooden structure. I pressed myself tightly into that corner and kept my eyes, from that point on, fixed on that miniscule sliver of light, completely mute the whole time. That little dot of light kept me sane throughout the ordeal.

Suddenly a voice, out of nowhere, asks, "Are you okay in there?"

A choir of angry, but relieved voices replied, "No. We're stuck."

A minute later, someone opened the door and we escaped to safety.

We'd had enough sightseeing for one day and headed back to our hotel. We walked to Chinatown for dinner that night and together enjoyed a variety of interesting dishes. It was difficult to eat, though, because we couldn't stop laughing as we relived those endless moments in the elevator—likely no more than ten minutes. The story got bigger and funnier with each telling and we laughed until copious tears salted our food.

I try to avoid elevators, preferring to take the stairs if the distance is not too great. And I still—always—in the darkness of everyday heartaches, loneliness and fears, indecisiveness, chaos and strife, try to keep my eyes fixed on the Light—the "Light that shines in the darkness—the Light of the world—Jesus."

Plain Jane

Beauty is—supposedly—in the eye of the beholder. That's why, when you look at yourself, you see a distorted image. Shakespeare said it this way, "The eye sees not itself but by reflection." We have well-lit, good mirrors today, but, often a flawed self-image. We either think too highly of ourselves or we see ourselves as "lowly worms," doormats for cleaning mud and doggie doo-doo off the bottom of others' shoes. Instead of looking in the right places, many of us tend to view ourselves through the critical eyes of those who see us unfavorably. When we look closely in those bright, magnified mirrors, then, we see ourselves through their eyes, enhancing every physical imperfection, every wart and wrinkle. I know my nose is too long, my chin too pronounced, my face too round—among other beauty defects. I've learned to be comfortable in my own skin and hair, though, but that hasn't always been the case.

Although I was older, I grew up in the shadow of my younger sister—the beloved baby in the family. Not only was she smart and talented, she was really cute and cuddly, too. Out of the five girls in our family, only she inherited warm chestnut colored hair that was soft and smooth. Mother would braid her long locks, put her hair up in a bouncy ponytail or twist it elegantly into a bun on top of her head. As she grew older, her hair seemed tailor made for the era—the 1960s—and she wore her hair long, straight, and sexy—and her skirts, short. I suppose you wouldn't be surprised to know that she was really well-liked—especially by the boys!

I was born bald. If you flipped me over, you wouldn't be able to tell the top from the bottom—both were smooth and hairless. When I finally grew some hair on my head it was pale—very blond, coarse and naturally wavy. For some unknown reason, my mother liked playing with my hair, too. But instead of trying to smooth out those rebellious locks, she'd set my hair with curlers—actually, rags. Rag curls found a welcoming home in my hair. So much so, that when the rags were removed you couldn't tell it—the curls stayed tight to my head—as if they were giant bee stings, or blond boils that had sprouted all over my head. Her favorite time to practice with those rag curls, of course, was the night before the annual school picture. Normally my hair flew wildly around my head, I wish I could say "like a halo" but that would be a lie. My hair was coarse and bushy and unbecoming. I envied Clara her smooth, straight hair.

When I was about twelve, I convinced my mother to give me a home perm. Home perms were powerful potions in those days and this one was no exception. The perm took. It took magnificently. Within two days I couldn't get a comb or a brush through the tangles—my hair had become a jungle. Too embarrassed to say anything, I'd just lightly comb the few straggly loose outer hairs, hoping to camouflage what lay beneath. Standing in the lunch line at school one day, two of the "tough girls" behind me surprised me by their sudden interest in me—I honestly think it was the only time they ever even spoke to me—as they asked, "Did you get a perm?"

"Yes," I'd replied, tossing my head slightly so they could admire my stylish new hairdo. I wondered why they'd smirked and rolled their eyes.

A few days later, while my eldest sister Jennie and her then husband, Bill, were visiting, I sat contentedly beside my mother, enjoying the camaraderie of the moment with various family members. Mother started to play with my hair, quickly stopped and exclaimed in horror, "What on earth did you do to your hair, Lela?"

I blushed beet red and whined plaintively, "I can't get the brush through it." My hair was so tangled by this time you could almost lift my shoulder length hair in one solid mass.

For the next hour—or two—I sat there in total humiliation as my mother meticulously, painstakingly removed the "rats" one-by-one from my hair. My brother-in-law threw back his head and roared with laughter throughout the process. I adored Bill but I wasn't laughing; it was not an enjoyable few moments in my life. And I never, ever got a perm again.

On another occasion, a year or so later, I'd begged my busy mother for several weeks to trim my bangs which were hanging in my eyes. After listening to me whine and complain, teasing her incessantly, she'd finally had enough. My normally unflappable mother sat me down and began to trim those bangs. She was visibly annoyed. Instead of snip, snip, snip, the sound a delicate pair of scissors might make, I got the distinct impression that I was a doomed chicken and my mother, who had decapitated many a plump fowl in her day, was actually wielding an axe or a meat cleaver in her hands. I could see by her expression that her anger had abated somewhat as she gazed in wonder at her completed handiwork.

I got what I wanted. She had trimmed my bangs—basically into non-existence. Those bangs were so short they stood up like the bristles on a toothbrush. They say the only difference between a good haircut and a bad one is two weeks. But I couldn't stay home from school to wait for those bangs to grow out. I put on a brave face and headed off to school. I noticed a lot of second looks but only my friend Debbie, gazing at me in rapt fascination, had dared asked, "Did you cut your bangs, Lela?" Duh!

When I was sixteen I visited a genuine beauty salon for the very first time and my mother never again cut my hair after that. Because my hair was thick, I generally wore it short but my anxiety level over my hair didn't diminish easily.

I was wearing my hair short when I met my husband. He didn't seem to mind my short hair but that was probably because he was looking at my long legs, visible beneath the style of the time, mini-skirts. One day, a year or two into our marriage, my hubby suddenly said to me, "I wish you'd let your hair grow." Since he'd never uttered a preference before, and moved by the longing in his voice, I made an immediate decision to acquiesce.

I suffered through the awkward in-between stage until my hair grew below my shoulders. My thick unruly mop of hair needed a lot of work to manage, so every night I would set my hair on huge rollers to bring order and style to it. No more quickie hairdos with the convenient blow dryer—a recent tool on the market and one I had learned to utilize. For all my efforts, though, my husband never seemed to notice. I did receive several compliments from other people, but the one person I desperately yearned to hear from remained silent.

After a couple of years, constantly struggling with my hair, I finally ask my husband if he minded if I got my hair cut. He shrugged. "Whatever you want," he said disinterestedly. That sounded like a green light to me and I filed the information away for possible future use.

Later that summer, friends of ours asked us if we'd be willing to be their substitutes for a bowling team they were on. They bowled on a league team made up of four people that required at least two substitutes. Neither of us had really ever bowled—once or twice was all. My initial experience had been a negative one, with my date sarcastically telling me that I "looked funny" in my approach. Every time I stepped up to the lane to roll my ball, my mind hit the instant replay button as I imagined everyone watching me, probably laughing because I "looked funny." Needless to say, feeling that insecure did not make me want to jump at this opportunity. They assured us that we'd rarely need to fill in, though, and as they were all avid bowlers I reluctantly agreed.

About three weeks into the season, we got a call. My heart dropped into my stomach as I heard this news, "Debbie had to have emergency surgery. She's going to be out of commission for a while. We need you to bowl for a few weeks."

Although we were friends with Vic and Kathy, it wasn't a close relationship and I quickly got the impression that bowling was very serious work and highly competitive—especially for Kathy. She was a good bowler. "My average is around 155-160," she pompously informed me after my second or third frame of gutter balls. She was smiling but there wasn't any warmth in it. Her eyes were on a distant trophy which appeared to be in jeopardy. I gritted my teeth, straightened my shoulders and inwardly vowed I would not drag this bowling team into the gutter with me. Thankfully, I only needed to get through a few weeks and I could do that. I *would* do it I silently promised myself.

Several weeks passed. We were bowling every week and I was carefully watching the other bowlers and working on my technique. Whenever we ask about Debbie's return, we were met with ambiguity—her recovery seemed slow. The weeks continued to accumulate. I began to almost enjoy the sport and my average started inching up—70s, 80s, 90s.

One day part way through the season, I decided that this was the day—the day to cut my long hair, that is. Fortunately, when I called my hairdresser, Louis, he had an opening and could squeeze me in that very day. Those are the kind of decisions you have to act on quickly or you might change your mind.

When my husband arrived home, dinner and I were both waiting. I looked like a new woman and almost dared to feel attractive with my new short coif. I was eagerly anticipating my husband's response. "How was your day?" I asked, as if it were a normal day, all the while dying inside to ask what he thought of my hair. But, I stayed silent, afraid to broach the subject.

He kinda' grunted, "It was a day." With the fragrance of one of his favorite meals tickling his nose—a deliberate tactical maneuver—I tried positioning myself so he would have a more flattering view of his stylish wife. But after an initial quick perusal, he avoided looking directly at me. I felt a small spark ignite in the depths of my spirit and we began a game of cat and mouse that would continue throughout the evening.

It was bowling night. When I stepped up to the lane and sent my bowling ball spinning down it, I was hot—fuming inside—and dead on accurate. Strike. He stepped up and hurled his ball toward those pins standing at attention—as if they were enemy soldiers—strike. War had been declared. We both bowled our best games that night, games we would earn trophies for at the banquet at the close of the season. Yep. We ended up bowling the entire season. My average continued to climb throughout the year and I also earned a pin for the most improved women's average, a small vindication of sorts.

Many years later when I began working toward a degree, I took a bowling class as my required P.E. credit. Once again, I received a trophy—this time for the best woman's average—and had my picture taken for the college bulletin board. That year of painful struggling had prepared me for the challenge—at least in bowling.

My husband never did comment on my hair. I'd periodically let it grow and cut it off again several times through the years. Occasionally he might make a general denigrating observation about women and short hair—but never specifically addressed mine. Since it appeared that I was dammed either way, I eventually gave up and settled on a style that worked for me—short! He'd once told me that I was a "Plain Jane" which might seem like an insult to you, but he went on to qualify his comment, "What you see, is what you get." His comment had hurt my feelings at the time, but in retrospect, I considered it a kind of compliment. I am who I am—Plain Jane—and quite comfortable being so. Scripture tells us that man judges by the outward appearance and God looks at the heart. My shell *is* plain and that's okay. I pray that the essence of me is made up of beautiful characteristics: love, joy, peace, patience, kindness, goodness, faithfulness, gentleness—and—a bit of self-control.

A Woman's Destiny

As I was preparing dinner one summer afternoon, the telephone rang. "This is Lela," I said.

Without even a "Hello" the voice on the other end asked, "Are you going to be home for a while? We'd like to stop in for a few minutes. "

"Why don't you come for dinner?" I responded.

About five minutes later my daughter and granddaughter appeared at our door. Our eight year old granddaughter, Elizabeth, excitedly flounced in, obviously expecting some specific response from us. Although she had wanted to donate her long beautiful locks to charity earlier in the year, the hairdresser had not cut quite enough to meet the requirements. On this day her mother had taken her to the salon for a stylish new hairstyle, the shortest haircut she'd ever had, and she needed some masculine admiration. That's what a good "Pop" is for and my husband, an expert at flattery and praise, more than satisfied her fragile ego.

Elizabeth is an introspective, mystical young lady. Although she's fond of frogs and caterpillars, she *loves* fantasy and dress-up, art and dance, music and romance. To match those interests, she comes ready-made with a super sensitive and highly temperamental personality, providing our family with some colorful moments—especially since our other three grandchildren are all "clueless" boys.

When Elizabeth comes for a sleepover, she totes along a menagerie of stuffed toys and dolls, goes into the guest room and proceeds to spend an hour "setting up" her space. After bathing, brushing her teeth, enjoying a few books read aloud and prayers sent heavenward, she has, on occasion, covered her hair with a nightcap and when settled in bed, placed eye shades over her eyes as if she were a glamorous beauty queen.

Every year before school starts, her doting grandparents take her shopping for new clothes. Pop helps choose potential outfits and I go with her into the "changing room" as she calls it, to try everything on. Elizabeth usually wants a few accessories to complement her outfits, too, so almost every new shirt and pants, or skirt, must also be modeled with a hat—or some other accessory. She admires herself from the front, the side, and, sometimes, even the backside! It's a hoot watching her unselfconsciously watching herself wiggling her butt. This year, she and her mother had spent several days at the beach, so Elizabeth took a few moments between each outfit to admire her tan—from every angle, of course! It's quite an excursion, this shopping with Elizabeth. (Some different than her mother who HATED shopping.)

On our way to the car, Elizabeth decided we needed to make one more stop, and without conferring with us, she entered an accessory shop to look for earrings with her well-trained and faithful followers at her heels. She waltzed up to the clerk and asked if they had any "clip-on" earrings. While she's spinning the rack, I firmly tell her—in my feeble attempt to exercise some small measure of authority—that we are not buying her any earrings. She didn't complain, however, but graciously accepted our refusal. As we walked away, I attempted to sell her on the idea of pierced ears. "Why don't you get your ears pierced?" I asked her. "It's so much easier, and think how many more choices you'd have."

"It'll hurt too much," she insists. "Mommy said so."

"Only at first," I reply. "You just have to clean them faithfully."

Elizabeth adamantly shakes her head, "You're not convincing me. Aunt Jennie wears clip-on earrings and I'm going to, too."

We agree we'll let it go for now and we head for home.

Anyway, the day after her new haircut, I'm expecting all three of my young grandchildren for the day: Elizabeth, Daniel, who is also eight years old, and his brother, three-year-old Matthew. Knowing how sensitive Elizabeth can be, I had asked my daughter, Andrea, to prepare her boys for Elizabeth's new hairdo. The boys arrived at my house about one-half hour before Elizabeth, and I, too, spent some time making sure they were prepared to make her feel beautiful. "Now, don't forget to tell Elizabeth that her hair looks nice," I remind them as my chronically late younger daughter, Sarah, dropped Elizabeth off at the front door and whizzed away. I hurried to greet her, Matthew close behind me. "Hi, Elizabeth," I said to my smiling granddaughter whose stylish new hairdo had a few added waves from a night's sleep.

Without missing a beat, Matthew obediently and diplomatically said, "I like your hair, Elizabeth."

The smile disappeared behind a big, dark thunder cloud, and with hands on her hips, Elizabeth fairly spat at me, "You told them," then rushed into the bathroom, slammed the door and stayed sequestered there for several long minutes.

Matthew looked at me in complete bewilderment. Daniel, a more seasoned companion to his temperamental cousin, stayed clear of the entire subject, wisely waiting for the dust to settle before attempting to engage Elizabeth in conversation.

Apparently, Elizabeth had expected her two young cousins to notice and be razzle-dazzled by her new hairdo. Dream on, Elizabeth. We ladies rapidly learn most guys are completely clueless in the area of fragile female diplomacy. At the ripe old age of eight, I'm proud to report, Elizabeth is already efficiently fulfilling her pre-ordained, God-given female destiny—that is, to make the world a more stimulating, mysterious and challenging experience for everyone!

Time: Watching and Waiting

Watching and waiting. That's what most mothers, grandmothers and, eventually, daughters spend much of their time doing—waiting at the doctors, the dentist, at the bus stop, music, dance, or swimming lessons. We wait for a phone call, a visitor, a teenager out on a date, or our husbands to get home for dinner, anxiously pacing the floor from window to door and back again. Most of us remember the endless waiting to become a teenager, to drive a car or graduate from high school. Through the long, dark days of winter, we eagerly wait for the sun's return to the northern hemisphere, then, a few months later, we are watching for the first, feather flakes of white to come drifting down. We watch both clock and calendar intently. Sometimes the hands of the clock don't move at all, sitting in a boring classroom, or listening to an uninspired speaker drone endlessly on. Waiting for Christmas can look like forever to a little person counting the days on the calendar. But, more often, time whizzes by so fast you are left breathless by the journey, realizing that you had missed the trip, wondering how you arrived at the destination.

Besides those moments when we physically wait, however, are those more subtle anticipatory instances intrinsically tied to our emotional health: waiting for love, for knowledge, understanding, wisdom, satisfaction, peace, acceptance, validation, vindication, or victory. Time moves as if it were a river—slow, lazy, tranquil in various places, and, at other times, we are swept up in the swift current, propelled effortlessly, often helplessly, perhaps even reluctantly, downstream toward our final destination—invisibly becoming a part of the vast, deep blue sea of souls, the end of this life as we know it. If our sojourn here has been a long, arduous path, we wait with faith and hope for the next chapter—a better chapter, the grand finale or what we as followers of Jesus Christ call Heaven.

Our culture is a slave to time; we are ruled by it. We look at life in linear fashion, moving along a straight line from points A to Z, orderly and predictable, and we like it that way. (Maybe we just think we like it because we've been trained that way.) Other cultures, unless contaminated by our neuroses, recognize the value of living in the present moment. The indigenous "first peoples" saw life in a cyclical manner, a much less stressful way of living than the merciless time master who owns us. As my husband would say, "What goes around, comes around."

Not only do I have clocks in most every room in the house, I also wear a watch, check the microwave, my computer monitor, and the cable box attached to the television set for the time at periodic intervals. "What time is it?" is one of the most well-worn questions in our society. And, to further enhance the importance of time—I use the timer to ensure I'm using just the right amount of it.

Obviously, when you're baking cookies, it's smart to set the timer for ten minutes if the recipe so specifies. I prefer to slightly under-bake cookies so I'll adjust the time a bit, to maybe seven or eight minutes. I use the timer for most everything I cook or bake. I want perfection in my finished product.

I limit phone time, pleasure reading, short naps or computer time with the same tool. When the buzzer goes off, I terminate the conversation, close the book, open my eyes or walk away from the computer.

We utilize a woodstove all winter as supplementary heat. I set the timer to monitor how long to leave the dampers open to get the fire going properly. The timer works for charging the cell phone the correct length of time, too.

I have, on occasion, employed my timer when babysitting. Since spanking has been morally outlawed by politically correct society, I put my disobedient grandchildren in "time-out" as punishment. Yep. I set the timer for five minutes.

The summer Matthew was three, he defiantly disobeyed me. He reacted indifferently to a strong word spoken to him as if it were a tiny annoying gnat. Matthew believes he was divinely wired to rule his world, including any who may venture in, regardless of size, age or gender. After several attempts to negotiate, I finally sat him in a chair in the large hallway at the base of my steps, facing a hall piece with a mirror and hooks to hang coats on. I placed the timer strategically, where he could watch its progress. "There. I'm setting the timer for five minutes," I told him as he watched me turn the dial.

"Ahhhhhhhhh," he yelled angrily, kicking his legs in protest, not caring if there might be consequences.

I picked up the timer and moved the dial. "That's one more minute," I said.

"Errrrrrrr," Matthew growled, arms and legs flailing wildly. You could visibly see his frustration. At that moment he'd have given anything to be much bigger and stronger.

I added one more minute to the timer. "Every time you complain," I tell him firmly, "you'll have one more minute added to your time."

How dare I impose those unjust restrictions? Once more his body went into ugly, defiant contortions as he loudly protested with his own version of sound effects, "Errrrrr. Ahhhhhh."

Silently I picked up the timer and moved the dial one more minute.

Matthew studied the vile object intently. He didn't move. He didn't utter a sound. For eight minutes he sat and watched the timer until the buzzer announced his freedom. I didn't have to use the timer again all summer. That doesn't mean Matthew abdicated his God-given role on this earth; he merely chose to use his abilities more discriminately. A wise leader in the making.

I frequently use my timer to remind myself that it is time to leave for some appointment, primarily these days to pick up a grandchild from school or the bus.

When Elizabeth was in first grade, she attended a school about two miles from my home. Due to her mother's work schedule, I picked her up twice a week that year. I would stand outside, lost in the crowd of other parents, grandparents and babysitters retrieving youngsters at the close of their day at school.

One Friday, a cold winter's afternoon, I stood alone in the crowd, shivering and hugging myself to keep warm, waiting for Elizabeth to be dismissed from school. When Elizabeth appeared, she scanned the crowd until she found me. Instead of making her way toward me, however, she momentarily disappeared. When she reappeared, Elizabeth was tightly gripping the hand of a tiny girl and seemed to be pulling her in my direction. Like me, Elizabeth is tall. Her little friend and fellow first-grader barely reached Elizabeth's shoulder. "This is my friend, Dakota," Elizabeth said to me.

"Hi, Dakota," I said smiling at this cute miniature person. Knowing my granddaughter, I should have suspected this was not some polite, chance meeting but a deliberately orchestrated moment.

Elizabeth was born with innate panache, that is, she knows how to dress *and* accessorize. Without any other small talk, Elizabeth dove straight to the purpose for this encounter. "Can you make her a scarf?" Elizabeth asked ingenuously. "She doesn't have one, and it's really cold." Like two hungry puppy dogs they stood looking up hopefully at me. All that was missing were two tongues hanging out and a pair of wagging tails.

"Hmmmm," I murmured thoughtfully, trying to buy myself some time.

"Please, Nani?" Elizabeth begged.

"I guess, I can do that," I replied cautiously. How could I say no to two sets of puppy dog eyes?

That was all she needed to hear. "Bye, Dakota. See you Monday." And we went our separate ways.

As we walked to my car, though, Elizabeth wanted to seal the deal and efficiently picked up the thread while it was still hot. "When can you make it? She really needs a scarf. Could you do it this weekend?"

I gulped in astonishment. "This weekend?" I asked, my voice squeaking a little, mentally sorting through my weekend calendar.

She had tremendous confidence in me, faith that, of course, I would be both willing and able to meet her expectations. I'm her grandmother, after all. "It's really cold," she added persuasively, in case I had any residual doubts about this high-priority philanthropic request.

"I'll try," I nodded in response. In Elizabeth's mind it was a done deal.

I studied my crochet books, tried a couple of patterns, and finally settled on a design that worked fast. I delivered the finished scarf to my daughter on Sunday and Elizabeth took it to school with her on Monday.

Tuesday afternoon I was once again waiting in the cold, blustery shadows of the tall brick building. When Elizabeth appeared, she once again had Dakota by the hand and was dragging her friend down the sidewalk toward me. Dakota's neck was stylishly wrapped in her new colorful scarf. Elizabeth gave her friend a gentle push. "Now," Elizabeth ordered imperiously, "tell my Nani, thank you."

Dakota looked up at me, a very long distance for this diminutive, little person, and shyly said, "Thank you." She didn't really have any choice, of course. Elizabeth, the consummate mother/caregiver/boss gave Dakota her blessing with a warm hug and we parted ways. The next week, my daughter Sarah, who is also Elizabeth's mother, handed me a sweet, hand-written thank you note from Dakota. I imagine Dakota didn't have any options in that thank you, either. Some of us are just naturally meant to rule and some of us spend our lives saying, "Okay. Sure. Yes, dear. Whatever you say."

I don't really mind waiting. In a way, waiting forces time to be your servant, rather than vice versa. Waiting balances movement. "Wait for the Lord . . ." Scripture reminds us. "Be still," the psalmist wrote, "and know that I am God." If we use our waiting time appropriately, then, we should get to know God really well. And who knows, rather we go of our own volition or are forced kicking and screaming into those periods of waiting, we may just discover character building opportunities in those "time-out" moments; opportunities for reflection, inner growth, and/or acts of unselfish kindness. I know this, and celebrate . . . "my times are in His hands."

The Club

When Sam graduated from high school, we collectively breathed a sigh of relief and inwardly celebrated the success of a long, challenging journey. Some people are natural students and Sam demonstrated his love for information early on in his scholastic sojourn. Although he loved stories, it was science and history that piqued his interest most. Even before he could read, he'd spend hours entrenched in books about archeology, ancient history, geology, weather, insects, pirates and cowboys and Indians. Then, once he mastered the skill of reading, he would disappear into the bathroom for long stretches of time, book in hand, to absorb information while he discharged waste—a habit he never lost. But, while many people need stories to fuel their imagination, Sam, who was wonderfully creative, could conjure up a marvelous adventure from the barest of facts, basically *ex nihilo*. He effortlessly entertained himself for hours. That's why we were all a little surprised that he struggled as a student.

For all of his early school years, I would pick him up at school and keep him for the next couple hours until his mother was done working for the day. That meant that I had to do his homework with him. He would sit on a barstool at the kitchen counter addressing his assignments while I was prepping for dinner. Homework was a huge challenge. Many kids might lose their focus between sentences—or, perhaps, between spelling words, e.g., *finish* and *frequent*. Sam mentally drifted off between *letters* in his spelling words, for example, *f* and *r*. And, while he was supposed to be doing an assignment, he often paused to watch what I was doing—besides prodding him to finish his work and frequently assisting him, that is. Once, as I was peeling potatoes, he watched me finish one and put it in the pot of water. "Can I put the next one in?" he asked.

"Of course," I replied. "But you have to do another problem, first." Sam bent to his work resolutely. When he completed the problem I handed him a peeled potato, he held his hand high and dropped that thing in the pot with a resounding and satisfying— SPLAT! One bomb had hit the target. Several potatoes later, with the enemy successfully annihilated, a happy boy returned to the drudgery of homework.

Every day I waited with other grandparents, parents and/or babysitters in a specified area as the school kids were dismissed. There usually was an impressive crowd although most students rode the buses. I'd watch as the first children began coming down the hall. No Sam. The trickle became a steady stream as many students hurried toward their waiting parents. No Sam. The stream dwindled back to a trickle and finally, among the last stragglers, Sam ambled unhurriedly down the hall, a decided air of distraction encompassing him. His shirt tail hung out over his pants, papers that had been carelessly stuffed in his backpack dangled precariously in many directions.

After greeting him I'd always ask, "How was your day, Sam?"

If he bothered to reply at all, his normal response was a disinterested and noncommittal, "Okay." It was obvious he had more important things on his mind.

However, one day when I asked, "How was your day?" he gave me a more detailed answer.

"I figured out how to get to the next level in Pokemon," he said, with a bit more enthusiasm than usual. Apparently Sam, an avid Nintendo devotee, had spent most of the day at school mentally conquering a challenge in his latest game! No wonder his teachers often got frustrated with him. He might have appeared to be physically present in class, but he likely was off somewhere more exciting, accumulating mental "frequent flyer" miles.

When Sam was in the second grade he started his own club. As his teacher explained to me, it was some kind of a "magic" club and was comprised of six young boys amenable to Sam's leadership. Everyone but "Charlie," that is. Every day as Sam and I rode the six miles home from the school to my house, I'd try to engage Sam in discussion. Besides "How was your day?" I might ask more specific questions like, "Did you pass the spelling test?" or "What did you do at recess?" (Besides lunch, recess was his favorite subject.) Although Sam is a talker, he is not very communicative about things he's not particularly interested in. But, for a brief time he passionately communicated about his club. Well, basically he passionately complained. He complained every day for a week about Charlie. It seems Charlie just didn't get it. All the other boys understood the rules of this club—unspoken or otherwise. Being a natural preacher, as most grandmothers are, I never wasted an opportunity to try and teach Sam a life lesson. And so, after several days of silent listening, I finally succumbed to that divine call and told Sam he *must* find a way to make Charlie feel as if he were an authentic part of his club. Sam, an introspective "old soul," appeared to understand what I was trying to say, but offered no audible response.

The next day I watched as Sam came slowly shuffling down that hallway, head drooping, shoulders slumped, his whole body language silently screaming dejection. No need to ask about this day. I gave his head a gentle caress and quietly walked him to my car. Once we were settled and on our way, I thought I'd cheer him up by asking about his latest passion, "How's your club, Sam?"

"I'm not in the club," he replied despondently.

"How can you not be in the club?" I asked in surprise. "It's your club."

Sam sadly answered, "I let Charlie make the rules and he kicked me out of the club."

I had to struggle to keep my composure but I couldn't help but mentally chuckle. As I mulled over that little exchange, though, I almost gasped at the profound implications of those words. I believe that the Creator of the universe bestowed on us an incredible gift—called life—then surrounded us with the beauty of the natural world in which to grow and blossom. Yet, with all the privileges and opportunities for living an abundant life we are blessed to enjoy, we chose to relegate the Creator to the fringes of our lives, opting to make our own rules and nonchalantly evicting him to a remote place, somewhere accessible, of course, in case we found ourselves in a tight spot—yet, out of the club.

Looking, but Not Seeing

I don't know if I've always been a skeptic but as I've matured physically, I've certainly lost my childlike sense of wonder. Having experienced my share of the miraculous, I'm confident that the invisible world is as real as the visible. Why, then, do I doubt? Nothing is simple for me. Like so many others, I want to know why and I want it to make sense. I can identify with the Israelites wandering in the desert. It didn't matter how many miracles God paraded in front of them, they still whined and complained about every hard or uncomfortable situation they were confronted with. They were fed, delivered, guided, and yet never satisfied. Promised a beautiful home—by the Creator of the universe, no less—but so subservient to their fear and discontent, they inadvertently sabotaged their golden opportunity for an abundant life.

Well, I was occupying an earthly "Promised Land" of my own. We had bought a piece of land with a beautiful view of the magnificent Delaware Water Gap and built a home on it. The house resembled an old farmhouse inside, and I always said I wanted visitors to feel as if time had stopped when they entered our home—and many did—or so they said. Most of the landscaping was done by our elderly handyman and dear friend, Bill Pugh. He chose various plants to dress up the grounds: rhododendron, azaleas, various yews and a variety of trees. Unfortunately, we live in heavily occupied whitetail deer territory—or, as my brother Dan more aptly observed about those critters, "They're nothing more than wild goats." Many of the beautiful shrubs would become casualties of those grazing "goats" but, thankfully, a few of our plants, like the rose bush, escaped unharmed.

I had let Bill decide what plants he wanted—except—I'd insisted that we needed a rose bush. I had in mind an old-fashioned pink rose bush similar to the ones that grew at home on the farm. But Bill had his own ideas and he sent me—with very specific instructions—to the nursery to pick one up. "I want you to get a climbing red rose bush," he said. "This is very important," he stressed firmly, looking me straight in the eye, "make sure it's Scarlet Blaze." (I'm not sure, even now, if I have the name correct.) He repeated the name of it again, just to make sure I had it right. Naturally, I blew it. I bought a climbing red rose bush but I only got the name half right. Although he was visibly annoyed, he planted the bush anyway.

It's kind of like sending a kid to the grocery store for a couple items and by the time they get there, their imagination has carried them to faraway places and they wonder what it is they're supposed to be purchasing. My mother once sent my sister, Clara, to the corner store for a bag of sugar. When she got there she asked the owner, Mr. Bullock, for 5 lbs. of lard. "Are you sure she wants 5 lbs. of lard?" he asked in puzzlement.

"Yes," Clara had confidently answered. "I'm sure."

He still wasn't convinced. "Maybe I should call your mother," Mr. Bullock worried aloud.

"No, I'm positive it's 5 lbs. of lard she wants."

Mother had laughed and kept the lard, and sent Clara scurrying back for sugar.

The wrong rose bush liked living at our house and it bloomed gloriously every year. I loved the rose bush, too, but, as time passed, I still longed for some old-fashioned pink roses, a yearning I frequently expressed to both my husband and my mother. One spring, after several years had gone by, the longing became especially intense. I fully intended to see about acquiring one. As with many good intentions, though, the busyness of life stymied my plans.

At the time I was the director of women's ministries at my local church and early that spring the district director of women's ministries in my denomination called and asked if I'd be willing to "do" the memorial service at our annual district convention in June. I said, "Yes." A short time later, when I sat down to assemble my thoughts and information, I realized that convention that year fell on the exact 35th anniversary of my father's funeral—June 4th.

I was only seven when my father died of a massive heart attack. As young as I was the trauma of that experience left an indelible impression on me. It altered my entire world. Next to the youngest of seven children, I spent those first seven years in an idyllic world—a world of hundreds of acres of woods and fields, pastures and ponds; a place occupied by lots of cows and chickens, several pets, and a large network of family and friends. At least four generations had preceded me in this little corner of the planet, and I'd actually been born at home, in a house built by my great-grandfather. I innately understood— even at my young age—that I belonged in this place. In one almost imperceptible, but cataclysmic moment in time, my life swiftly and ruthlessly changed its course.

I once heard someone attempt to describe death as a simple change of realities. For example, instead of driving the car all the way to your destination, you get out and walk the rest of the way. Or, while rowing a boat out on a lake, you decide to swim to shore. Even now, after many years of living, I cannot fully comprehend the complexities of life and death. Certainly living on a farm I had seen both new life—and death. But this was my first "people" experience and I wondered . . . what is death? What does it mean?

I don't remember much about the events surrounding my father's death—but—I will never forget the funeral. My father's funeral was held in the little United Methodist Church where he had served as Sunday school Superintendent for many years. I saw this pallid, expressionless figure lying still in a casket in front of the altar without actually comprehending the reality. Just a few brief weeks before, I had sat in this same church watching my father lead the opening exercises at Sunday school, gently rocking back and forth on his feet, dressed neatly in his Sunday best. He was wearing his Sunday best on this day, too. Everyone seemed so sad—many crying. I loved my daddy but I couldn't really grasp what had happened; nor did I understand their sorrow, only that it made me sad, too. I felt tears fill my eyes and I cried—for them, all the sad people—from the comfort and security of my mother's side.

The weather on that June day was perfect, bright sunshine and a cloudless blue sky. The sweet fragrance of roses permeated the air as they carried my father's coffin to its final resting place, next to my paternal grandparents in the cemetery adjoining the church. I remember two well-dressed ladies, strangers to me, standing near and talking to each other about my younger sister and me—as if we weren't there. "They'll forget," one of them said.

The other agreed. "They're so young."

I vehemently vowed to myself, "I will never forget." I didn't, of course.

Anyway, all those memories came flooding back as I worked on my eulogy for this convention and I decided I would mention my father in my service. The day of the convention I spoke briefly of some of the ambiguities surrounding death, my own early experience, and read the list of decedents—those members from throughout the district who had passed away during the past year—and then added, "And for my father, Lee Gillow." I closed by reading one of my father's favorite poems—a poem my mother had considered using at his funeral, then opted not to—*Crossing the Bar,* by Alfred Lord Tennyson.

A few days after the convention I walked outside and stopped to admire my rose bush, covered with glorious red blooms. I caught my breath in wonder. Right in the middle of that rose bush grew a branch of single old-fashioned pink roses, delicate and, oh, so sweetly fragrant. I lifted my arms in praise, feeling suffused with love. I was going through one of those prolific hard patches in life and was beautifully reminded that there is another reality existing concurrently—a wiser, kinder, both immanent and transcendent reality.

There's a couple of interesting footnotes to this story. First, I was amazed to find that many visitors or family members paused to admire my beautiful rose bush, yet never noticed the branch of pink roses until I pointed them out—a graphic picture of our learned response to stimuli—we often look with a cursory, hurried glance, seeing only what we expect to see, not bothering to pause for a closer look.

Then, however, there are those who choose to look for scientific explanations for this—and other—phenomena. I'm normally one of them. However, while recognizing that there often may be logical explanations, the timing is suspect. I had been longing for pink roses, thinking of my father, suffering through a hard place, and eulogizing departed souls. I might not have noticed the pink roses myself had I not been spiritually prepared.

Finally, there is this . . . a few days after I discovered my surreal gift I sat out on my daily walk. Walking briskly on our rural road and just out of sight of our home, I heard loud thrashing and crashing in the woods. Alarmed, I stopped, heart palpitating thunderously and found myself face to face with a big black bear. We both froze, staring silently at one another for what seemed like forever before both of us turned back—running this time—in the direction from which we had come. We scared each other! Before I reached our driveway, however, my brain unthawed enough for reason to return. I paused and said right out loud, "Lela, God wouldn't send you pink roses on your red rose bush only to let a bear attack you a few days later." I turned around and enjoyed an incident free two mile walk, keeping an eye and ear tuned to the woods, of course.

My rose bush still blooms; it's a pink rose bush now. Several small red blooms briefly appear at the base of the bush every year, the only reminder that this was once a rose bush of another color. I got my old-fashioned pink rose bush after all. And my faith—once again—got miraculously reinforced. I wonder . . . how many mystical moments, miraculous events or ethereal blessings have I missed throughout my life because I looked but didn't see, listened but didn't hear and/or let myself be ruled by skepticism, doubt, fear, cynicism or the mundane busyness of daily responsibilities?

Carpe Diem

I was babysitting my two young grandsons, Daniel and
Matthew, one hot summer day. Eight-year-old Daniel is a
sensitive soul who internalizes his stress, carrying the weight of
the world on his tender shoulders. The stress his mother feels,
he feels. The frustration his older brother expresses, Daniel
blames himself for. It doesn't seem to matter who it is creating
or expressing the problem, Daniel adds that straw to his already
overflowing load of burdens. And he desperately wants to make
it all okay—for everyone. To the discerning eye and attuned
ear, Daniel's insecurity appears obvious, as if emblazoned in
neon lights via his body language and/or facial expressions.

Matthew is an entirely different story. Matthew is three, two
months short of four, but already he would rule the world. Your
stress or unhappiness merely annoys him, because, obviously,
his needs, wishes and desires are of primary importance. As
Daniel is arduously loading everyone's problems on his own
back, Matthew's right behind him, shovel in hand, making
sure he doesn't miss anything. Matthew unconsciously exudes
confidence; he is saturated, permeated, filled up to the brim
with it.

On this particular day, the boys had been busy doing their
own thing, Daniel working on a Lego creation, Matthew,
a more physical little person, energetically running around
from one activity to another. Without warning there came
an ineffable moment—an inexplicable lull—a pause in the
action. Time seemed to momentarily stop. Matthew quietly sat
down on the couch. Daniel, perhaps feeling lonely, bored, or

curious—or, maybe, preveniently drawn to this moment, left the kitchen table and joined us in the family room. He sat down on the sofa next to Matthew. Although Daniel is a very bright, scholarly young boy, he's a bit challenged with motor skills. As he started to fling his arm around his little brother for some sibling camaraderie, he accidently poked Matthew in the eye. Matthew immediately jumped up, mad as a hornet and began yelling at Daniel. Daniel, being Daniel, was devastated, and began vocalizing a logical explanation. "I didn't mean to. It was an accident. I just wanted to hug you," he's urgently telling the little brick wall.

The little brick wall wasn't interested. "Daniel poked my eye," he complained loudly. He's a wonderful whiner—actually, an expert at the craft.

It was time for a Nani [me] intervention. "Daniel didn't mean to hurt you," I tell Matthew firmly, in my best "no nonsense" voice. "You need to enjoy these summer days with Daniel because Daniel will have to go back to school before you know it." Turning to Daniel I ask, "How many more days before school starts? Do you know? Let's go check." Without waiting for a reply, I hurry to the kitchen, Daniel on my heels, to check the calendar. We count the weeks—five. Matthew follows us, climbing up on the barstool that Daniel is standing next to. "You see, Matthew. Daniel only has five more weeks before he has to go back to school."

Matthew's chin starts to quiver, his eyes swimming in tears. "But I don't want Daniel to go to school," he sobbed. "I'll miss him." He wrapped his arms tightly around Daniel's neck and clung to him. The little brick wall had been effortlessly penetrated.

Daniel, who has one of those angelic faces, a smattering of tiny, cinnamon freckles sprinkled across his round cheeks, his glasses, loosened by too many close encounters with his little brother, precariously perched on the end of his nose, instantly began to beam—as if someone had plugged in the Christmas tree. He hugged Matthew fervently, seizing this moment of unexpected affection. "I have to go to school," he repeats to his heartbroken brother. "But I'll come back. Daniel always comes back."

Matthew is quickly quieted by these assurances. Too quickly. Maybe he didn't completely understand the certainty of this impending trauma.

Daniel is not about to squander this priceless opportunity and picks up the thread. "Daniel has to go to school. But I'll come back. I won't be gone too long."

Matthew is not crying anymore. He looks at Daniel and asks with grave seriousness, "How many days?"

Daniel is a whiz with numbers. He knows this answer, but he appears to be mulling the question over in his mind. "Not too long." He pauses. "About 180," he answers with obvious satisfaction, almost suppressing the little grin trying to emerge.

Matthew is no dummy, either. Almost imperceptibly, his chin begins to quiver once again. "That's a lot," he replies despairingly.

Daniel is so thrilled to know that he is the recipient of such great love, he cannot help himself, he must keep plumbing the depths. "I have to go to school. But Daniel won't be gone too long."

I have a gut feeling that this refrain will become a manipulative mantra, uttered in times of quiet desperation by a sensitive, insecure little boy. I hope it produces.

Occasionally, an unexpected act of kindness or authentic concern makes all the difference—it signals hope to the parched spirit lost and wandering in the dry, desolate desert of self-imposed emotional exile.

"Carpe Diem, Daniel."

Apparitions and Bears

I tend to be oblivious to the world around me while I work at my various chores and duties. I'm either focusing intently on the task at hand, indulging in frivolous thoughts or profound contemplations, or, perhaps, best case scenario, I'm just very involved in an on-going conversation with God. Whatever is mentally transpiring, I'm easily startled. My mother, who occupied an apartment attached to the rear of our home for twenty plus years, could open her door, walk across the family room, (the only room in our entire house carpeted, all others are hardwood) appear in our kitchen and begin speaking to me as I worked at some job, only to see me throw up my arms in fright, and scream, "AHHHHH" at the top of my lungs. After several years of receiving this response, she finally learned to open the door, stick her head in the family room and call, "Lela" to prepare me for her entrance.

One pleasant Sunday afternoon, Mother and I enjoyed walking a few slow laps around my driveway. It's one tenth of a mile around, but steep on one side and a gentle slope on the other, a good little work-out, especially for a lady in her early eighties. After several laps, my mother decided she'd had enough and retired to the house. I opted to go a bit more, likely counting laps to achieve some inner goal.

We call our driveway, "The Circle," which it is. The circle surrounds a piece of land we call, "The Island." We planted spruce trees at the foot of the island—five of them—now towering safe havens for various birds. Across the top of the island, my hubby and our then handyman, Bill, had planted a large variety of plants: lilacs, flowering crabapples, forsythia, rhododendron, red maples and others. I loved the diverse plants and trees even as they grew tall and thick—so dense, in fact, that I rather sarcastically nicknamed it, "The Buchanan Nursery."

Anyway, walking provides a perfect opportunity for reflection and I was knee deep in mental ruminations as I sauntered solo around "The Circle." About the third lap, I came up the steep side, crossed the top of the driveway, paralleling "The Nursery," which effectively hid the approaching visitor, and came face to face with a huge black bear ambling contentedly across "The Island." I screamed, "AHHHHH" at the top of my lungs, throwing my arms up in fright. As startled as I was, however, that poor old bear, literally jumped, his back feet temporarily airborne in fear, and he galloped away as fast as possible. I inadvertently scared the bear and ruined his perfectly happy Sunday afternoon stroll through the "Circle—Island—Nursery!" I must be more intimidating than I realized.

I've had several close encounters with bears through the years—especially since they are attracted to backyard bird feeders. My mother learned to bring her feeder, which hung on a hook right outside her kitchen window, inside every night to stymie those nocturnal visitors. After my mother got her heavenly address, we decided to hang two feeders on a pole in the backyard to attract various birds. Instead of looking out my kitchen window at her empty apartment, then, I would focus on the lively activity around the feeders. The feeders dangled high above the ground but, invariably one of those curious—and hungry—critters, that is, a black bear, would sniff them out.

One day a bear meandered into the yard, batted the feeders until they tipped over and carried one in his huge paws out under the black walnut tree. Cecil went outside yelling loudly and waving his arms like a madman at the bear, which totally ignored him, sitting on his bum, munching unconcernedly on birdseed and suet. My hubby repaired the damage to the feeders and we hoped for the best, knowing that bears usually travel a circuit. With any luck we wouldn't see him again—at least not soon.

Cecil's friend, Bert, stopped by a couple days later to drop off some information for Cecil. Recounting the story of the bear's raid on the bird feeder to Bert, an avid hunter like my husband, he told me how to cure the pest of his taste for Buchanan birdseed. "A Game Warden once told me to put a round of buckshot in the backside of a marauding bear. You can't be too close, of course. You want it to sting a little but not do any damage."

A few days later, in the pre-dawn hours, the bear surprised us with a return visit. We were sleeping fitfully, as we often do at the close of a night's rest, and heard the disturbance in the backyard. We rushed to the window to see the big, black beast pawing at the feeders. I'll always treasure the image of a highly annoyed Cecil, hair standing up in pre-shower disarray, clothed only in his whitey tighties and brandishing his shotgun, successfully peppering the behind of that bear with a load of buckshot. The bear lumbered rapidly up over the hill, and although he visited our backyard again, he wisely cut a wide berth around the feeders, only giving them a brief longing glance as he wandered past on his way to less dangerous feeding grounds.

Bears were not the only startled or startling visitors to our domicile, however. I grew up listening to paranormal tales and had, myself, experienced several logic-defying instances of doubtful origin. I didn't dwell on or pursue encounters with that reality, but I did have a healthy respect for the invisible realm. Still, you're never quite prepared for one of those unexpected, mysterious moments to enter the world you think you know and have a measure of control over. I'm actually not normally too fond of surprises.

Cecil was away, hunting in Canada. Often when he went hunting, I'd have a special "date" with my grandson Sam. We'd go to dinner and then a movie of his choice. He must have been between eight and ten this time, and we traveled about thirty minutes south to see a *Star Wars* show and have dinner at our favorite Italian restaurant. Watching a movie Sam enjoyed was always a treat. He didn't merely watch; he lived it. Other people thought they were seeing Luke Skywalker barreling through the universe in his aircraft. Sam knew that *he* was actually the daring pilot. He couldn't sit still, even in the theater. Every intense action shot, Sam participated in, his body flinching with every blow of the enemy, mentally flying, dueling, sparring with his light saber—all successfully, of course.

Anyway, it was late when I dropped him off at his house. When I got home, I quietly went next door to see if my mother was awake. She was sleeping soundly so I turned the lamp off in her living room, a sign to her when she got up to pee, that I was safely home.

I wasn't sleepy so I sat down at my desk to work on some schoolwork. I was taking classes, then, preparing for the ministry. I was studying intently when I heard a strange noise—close by—a kind of rattling—the sound a paper bag might make. Slightly alarmed, I froze, listening with my whole self. Except for my eighty-something mother, I was alone in this big house and responsible for her well-being. I searched the general area, but that was it—just one forever unexplained rattle. Then the phone rang. Who could be calling at 11 p.m? Andrea—my daughter—Sam's mother. Just to talk. I swung around in my swivel chair, chatting cheerfully away. I now faced the long windows in the room I call my "Sanctuary." Imagine my reaction when an apparition silently appeared in one of those windows, dressed all in white, hair loose to its shoulders and flying about its face, arms waving. All that was missing from this spectral visitor was a ghostly "Ooooooh." Already a little spooked by the eerie rattling, I screamed "AHHHH" in outright terror and dropped the phone.

It's a wonder I didn't have a heart attack—or my unsuspecting mother either. She had awakened, seen my lights and wandered over to see me. Her hair floated in disarray around her face, and she was wearing a long, faded pink, almost white, flannel nightgown. She stood silently in the doorway to my sanctuary, prudently waving her arms at me so I wouldn't be frightened. She didn't realize I was facing the other way, staring at a distorted reflection of her in the window—a reflection that looked like the apparition my mind had predisposed me to via the late hour, the aloneness, the spooky rattling, and my innate sensitivity to surprise. How we laughed when we both recovered from our shock—a laugh we shared with every recounting in the years ahead.

I've enjoyed my share of supernatural experiences through the years—and even though they're a bit disconcerting, I'm okay with that reality. They usually don't make me laugh, however. My own human fallibility, on the other hand, can be side-splitting hilarious.

The Pool Party

As a tool of the trade as grandmother/babysitter I had purchased an inflatable pool about two feet deep and seven feet wide and filled it with water. It was meant to provide hours of enjoyment for my three young grandchildren.

One hot and humid summer day, a day rife with uneasy restlessness, I sat on the deck watching Elizabeth, Daniel and Matthew climb into the pool, hoping that the refreshing cool water would act as a panacea to the palpable discord. You'd think it would have been a carefree, happy experience but this is how it went . . . .

Almost immediately they felt the intrinsic need to establish some invisible rules and boundaries, and, more importantly, to figure out "who's in charge." Obviously, Elizabeth, a whole four months older than Daniel and the only girl besides, should inherit that role. Plus, we ladies are natural caretakers so it makes sense that we should have our say. Elizabeth wasted no time attempting to assert her seniority.

Her first observation, however, elicited this response from Daniel, who had been demonstrating symptoms of extreme contrariness all day. "Don't be negative," he said, parroting a refrain he hears repeatedly from me and immediately raising Elizabeth's hackles.

"I'm not being negative," she retorts hotly as they're all splashing in the water, physically getting acclimated to the water temperature and tentatively feeling their way toward a viable system of play, satisfactory to all the participants; "testing the water" so to speak, and bickering incessantly.

"Stop it."

"That's not nice."

"I was playing with that."

"I had it first."

"No, you didn't."

"Elizabeth's not being fair."

"Yes, I am."

The verbal sparring continues nonstop as they perform awkward gymnastics in the adequate but limited space. It is my turn for a little negativity, "You sound like a bunch of fussy old ladies," I tell them in exasperation.

Daniel, who has a stocky, very white body, decides to attempt laying on the wide rim of the pool to work on a tan. "I'm going to get a good tan, Nani," Daniel says to me, ignoring Elizabeth and Matthew. Elizabeth tells a conveniently deaf Daniel that he can't lie on the pool, but, although he wobbles a bit, he balances successfully in place for several minutes.

Matthew sees a golden opportunity and tries to dislodge the tantalizing target from its resting place. "Stop it, Matthew," Daniel yells. "Don't pull me into the pool if I'm not ready." Daniel is a huge worrier—about everything. "I hope we don't get too much vitamin D," he adds reflectively, again repeating a line I frequently use to get the kids to play outside. "There's a bee. Stay away from the bee," Daniel shouts, a note of panic in his voice. Matthew had recently experienced a painful close encounter with a bee, raising their awareness of the potential danger they posed.

"Owww. Stop kicking me."

"I didn't kick you."

"Yeah, you did. See, there's a bruise, right there," pointing to the faded remnants of an old wound.

"Ewwww. Look. There's a dead worm. Dead worms are gross." (All worms are gross in my opinion, but I chose not to get involved in this stimulating dialogue.) "It has a hole in its body," Daniel observes. "Maybe ants used it as a tunnel," he adds ingeniously, pretending to be oblivious to the others and deliberately boycotting the play overtures of Elizabeth and Matthew.

Although it's highly risky leaving them alone for even a few brief moments, nature cannot be denied any longer, and I make a mad dash to the bathroom. A quick perusal around my house reveals the remnants of a small tornado. There is underwear everywhere: on the kitchen floor, on the master bath floor, and in the downstairs half bath. Pink flowered underwear, Spiderman underwear, inside out, twisted underwear. In the master bath, the toilet seat—and lid—are both down—as Elizabeth has been taught. In the half bath, the toilet seat—and lid—are both up—as the boys prefer—it's so much faster and more convenient.

When I return, Elizabeth and Matthew are both wearing empty cool whip containers as hats. They fill the containers with water and then invert them on their heads, water cascading down over them, creating a human waterfall. She's teaching him her own version of a little song . . . "I'm a pretty teapot . . ." They tip their heads and the cool whip containers fly into the pool and they laugh hysterically, as if it were the funniest thing in the world, an overt attempt to entice Daniel into joining them.

Daniel stubbornly persists at the impossible task of attempting to appear indifferent. As Elizabeth plops into the water with gusto, trying another tactic to engage her obstinate cousin in play, Daniel indignantly sputters, "You almost landed on me."

"No, I didn't."

"Yeah, you did. My legs were straight out."

"No, they weren't."

Matthew is tired of being left out of the fray. He's the most enthusiastic brawler in the bunch. He jumps on Daniel and they briefly wrestle before tumbling out of the pool onto the ground. "I almost passed out," Daniel complains. "I was unconscious," he grumbles crossly as they clamber back into the water.

I sit silently, notebook in hand, recording this fascinating glimpse into the conversation and interaction of the little people, chagrined to realize that they are unconsciously parroting more than mere words they've heard their adult role models demonstrate. There are all kinds of emotional undercurrents at work. I mediate only if absolutely necessary.

Matthew loves conflict. He's ready for more and lunges at his big brother. "Matthew, don't push me down. You could have kept me out for ten minutes," Daniel emphatically says, "or even a thousand years." A little hyperbole goes a long way. But, Matthew could care less. He's accomplished his goal. There's not much that pleases Matthew more than annoying Daniel.

"Let's have a jumping contest," Elizabeth suggests, in another obvious female ploy to bring harmony to the pervasive discord.

This has not been a good day for Daniel and he's not about to accommodate anyone. "If there's not a prize, I don't want to play," he says.

"I'll give you a thousand dollars," coaxes Elizabeth.

"I just want the whole family room—and the chair," replies Daniel. Under Elizabeth's tutelage, they had spent the morning setting up playhouses behind chairs and in corners in my family room, using afghans and pillows and toys to make cozy little personal spots—and arguing every minute about who got what and where.

As much as she wants harmony, though, that price is too steep for Elizabeth and she quickly decides to divert attention. "We're not going to have any more contests," she declares. "We're just going to have fun."

My chronically cantankerous grandson—on this day— stubbornly refuses to be happy. "This is not fun," he states. "Anything I can think of is not fun. I'm getting out of the pool." Daniel exits the water but stands close by. "It's not fun. It hasn't been fun all day," he adds, his gloomy malediction on the day's events.

Elizabeth and Matthew agree and climb out of the pool.

Daniel chortles gleefully as he hops back in. "That was the perfect lure," he brags smugly, "now I've got the pool all to myself," thinking he has outsmarted us all. Elizabeth is visibly annoyed. However, it was to be a short-lived victory.

At that moment Pop arrives home and they all decide to get out of the pool for interaction more stimulating than with boring old Nani. Pop is boisterous, energetic, loud and exciting. Everyone wraps up in their colorful beach towels and Elizabeth comes to sit near me in a deck chair. The chair is a little too close to the edge of the deck, though, and we watch paralyzed as her chair teeters and tips and both she—and the chair—tumble over—a look of panic and surprise on her face—landing smack-dab in my oregano—a short but embarrassing trip. She suffers no breaks or bruises—except to her fragile ego, and the fragrance of the crushed oregano wafting upward is lovely. "Nani," she accuses me, "you set my chair too close to the edge." I am almost smiling, but solemnly and apologetically agree with her.

Pop only stays a few minutes—long enough to be the "good guy." He's brought an assortment of popsicles and they all choose their favorite—except—wonder of wonders—they all have the same favorite!

"I want that one."

"That's my favorite and I picked it first."

"You got to pick first last time."

"No, I didn't."

"It's not fair."

We waste a lot of good energy wanting everything to be fair, because, in this life, it just isn't. Except—if you BELIEVE—there is one redeeming place in life—that is, in the wide shadow of a cross. In that place of faith we all become equal; inequity ceases to exist. Efficacious love has done its job. "It is finished," He said . . . and forever reconciled the vast array of petty human differences.

Although at various times throughout the day I had stooped to bribery—"You'll get a treat if you play nicely . . ." and, threats—"You won't get a treat if you don't stop fighting . . ." all the diplomacy and eloquence I could muster could not successfully settle the constant disputes on that day. An aura of discord hovered over the little pool party. As an ambassador of peace, I failed miserably. You can only negotiate peace if there is willingness on all fronts to personally let go of stubborn pride or a selfish agenda. In every successful relationship or difficult situation, compromise, acceptance, tolerance, forgiveness, or discernment are the weapons that ultimately move us along on our endless quest for peace, harmony, personal validation and/or resolution. Humor helps tremendously, too, though, and I was highly entertained by the various dynamics of uncensored human nature, gender quirks, and differing personalities. Although peace remained elusive, I know that some distant day these three young people will look back and laugh at this memory because they love each other deeply, and love *is* the most powerful force in the universe.

My disconcerting epiphany? I saw a bit of me, that day, in each of them.

Mexican Adventure

Watching the news show one weekday morning, I heard the news reporter ask this question of the creator of various cartoon characters. "Out of all the characters you've created, who is your favorite?"

Without hesitating, he replied, "Yogi Bear, of course, because he was smarter than the avvv-err-age bear. And, you know, his pal BooBoo was his conscience," he added.

My husband is an alpha male, type A "Yogi Bear" personality: a smart, aggressive, high energy, take charge and do it heartily kind of guy. He's the one you call when everyone else has declared defeat trying to move the refrigerator out the door. "What do you mean it won't fit?" he'd likely ask in surprise as he organized the troops to maneuver it successfully through the too small space. What's a missing piece of doorframe anyway? A mere incidental.

He's just as stimulating behind the wheel of the car. He likes to "boldly go where no man has ever gone before." Cecil rarely asks for directions and never gets lost, only a little "misdirected" on occasion. And he consistently tries to point out in his own sweet way, the mistakes other drivers are making, believing it's his divinely ordained duty to do so. His particular pet peeve is to have someone cut him off. "Did you see that?" he'll ask me. "He deliberately cut me."

I'll commiserate with empathy. "He knew it was you. He was thinking, 'there's Cecil, I think I'll cut him.'" Sometimes when we're out and about, he gets a little too aggressive for my "peace at any price" nature and I pretend that I'm a hostage. If there is a sign posted which reads, "No Parking," Cecil knows it actually means, "No parking—except for Cecil." He is wired to think that rules are challenges and invariably rises to the occasion with great pleasure. "You understand why I nicknamed him, Yogi Bear, don't you?"

That's why, when he broached the subject of a trip to Mexico several years ago, I inwardly gulped but smiled and said, "That sounds lovely, darling," and immediately signed up for a class in conversational Spanish, since I knew I'd have to get him out of jail. The first question I asked my teacher was how to say, "I'm sorry." No, better make that, "I'm *very* sorry." *Lo siento mucho.*

We traveled to Cancun and checked into a beautiful hotel right on the coast for a brief five day stay. We didn't need to worry too much about our language skills as everyone seemed to speak a little English. For example, the waiter magnanimously taught us to say, *"La quenta, por favor,"* or "The check, please?" We quickly discovered that money would be a key player on this trip.

When we walked through the colorful marketplace in downtown Cancun, vendors industriously and passionately solicited our business. "Come in," they called in their refined English. "What the hell. Just like Kmart," they added enthusiastically, gesturing with their hands to enter their stalls.

A queue of taxis waiting for business made their home outside our hotel door. We hired a pleasant young man to shuttle us around. He spoke good English. He'd lived in Chicago for seven years—illegally, as he freely explained to us. "My kinda' man," my husband happily exclaimed. Jose cheerfully showed us around town and we enjoyed the easy conversation. We had a good rapport going so we let him talk us into being our unofficial guide, grateful that we'd found a painless and enjoyable way to see a bit of Mexico.

The next day, at our request, Jose took us down the road to see some of the Mayan ruins. He seemed to know a bit about the history, but I found my ears straining to hear what the tour guides were authoritatively saying as they led groups of people around these magnificent remains. We weren't sure at the end of the day, but it *did* seem the taxi price was a little steep. But, this was Mexico after all, and Jose had been an enjoyable companion and capable guide.

The various potentially volatile situations, I quietly and unobtrusively manipulated to the best of my ability—a fulltime, highly skilled occupation that I've enjoyed over the past thirty-five years. Since Cecil is Yogi Bear, that obviously makes me BooBoo.

The time flew and before you could blink we were headed to the airport, Jose at the wheel. We effusively assured Jose how much his help had enhanced our trip. We all felt a little sad saying goodbye. The sense of goodwill rapidly dissipated, however, when Jose told us his price for this short airport run. Little tendrils of smoke began seeping out of my husband's ears and nostrils. I was proud of his remarkable restraint as he diplomatically tried to negotiate the outrageous charges. He is not a man who likes to lose; and definitely not to be outright fleeced. Jose had us though and he knew it. We knew it, too. We were "rich" Americans. What was money to us anyway but an abundant commodity to share with those less fortunate?

I breathed a sigh of relief and a heartfelt prayer of thanksgiving when our plane was airborne. It's a stressful career being Yogi's conscience. I'm happy to report that I didn't have to utilize my elementary Spanish to get my husband out of jail. I **did** have to expend a bit of energy trying to get him to see the humorous side of our Mexican adventure, though. It was one of those times that I thought I was a lot funnier than he thought I was—actually, I don't think he did see the humor, the pain in his pocket was too fresh.

Our short trip was replete with entertaining experiences. We came home a lot poorer and a little wiser. My husband learned to speak a little Spanish, too—his own version, that is. Instead of *bano* for bathroom, he coined the phrase *el toilete*, a term he proudly uses, on occasion, yet today. And the last words we utter aloud to each other—every single night—are the Hispanic version of I love you . . . "*Te amo.*"

"*Mucho, Mucho, Mucho,*" the other one replies.

From my perspective as BooBoo, I think that's a pretty impressive perpetual souvenir for a Yogi Bear adventure in Mexico.

One of Those Days

It was the worst ice storm in twenty-five years (January 2005). The white birch in the front yard groaned ominously, the top branches, heavy with ice, scraping the ground. The rain beating incessantly against the aluminum siding of the house was loud, as if someone were pounding on the door, begging entrance. There *was* someone at the door. Who would dare be out and about in the midst of such wild weather? Only the young and fearless, of course: my daughter, my five-year-old granddaughter, my son-in-law, and their old dog—Puppy. It seems their power was out and they needed shelter. We hunkered down together to ride out the storm.

By morning the storm had passed. The sun came out, dressing the world in a dazzling display of diamonds, sparkling in every direction—an ethereal landscape fit for fairies and angels. The roads and sidewalks quickly began emerging beneath the warmth of the sun. The first casualty of the day . . . the white birch. I grieved as it fractured into splinters under the weight of the ice.

My husband trotted off to work. He is not deterred by wind or rain, snow or ice. He'd much rather brave inclement road conditions than the hazards of spending involuntary time with four generations of family in confined quarters—and a dog, besides!

I could hear my elderly mother stirring on the omniscient baby monitor, an invaluable tool in those years. I hurried over to her apartment that is attached to the rear of our house. I started her coffee, set out her morning meds, weighed her (monitoring any fluctuation in fluid), checked her blood sugar, administered her insulin, fixed her breakfast and hurried home.

My daughter and her husband were waiting for me. Their power was still off and they wanted to go home to check on things and retrieve clothes for the day. Would I mind watching Elizabeth for a couple hours?

Elizabeth, a bright and beautiful little girl, and one of the joys in my life, has a powerful streak of contrariness running through her veins. She wanted absolutely nothing to do with me on this morning. I tried to interest her in un-decorating the little Christmas tree gracing the coffee table in the family room. The miniature angels, bells, candy canes and gingerbread men had been irresistible to her small fingers throughout the holiday season. But, today, they were unappealing. I had things to do, however, so I put an appropriate movie in the VCR, left her temporarily entertained, and went next door to prepare my mother for her day.

My mother had a doctor's appointment scheduled for the afternoon and she needed some extra attention. After showering her, washing her hair, drying her off and applying lotion to her chronically dry, itchy skin, she started for the bedroom to get dressed, only to suffer an unexpected attack of diarrhea. So hurriedly (as much as possible) she had to change direction and head for the toilet, unfortunately, leaving a trail behind her. When both she and her house were back in pristine—or close to it—order, a load of laundry humming happily in the washer, I returned home.

My daughter was back by now, so I went up to shower and dress, confident that the little person in the house was content and safely occupied. Just as I got up off the toilet, ready to step into the shower and naked as the day I was born, I heard the pitter-patter of little feet and the bathroom door flew open. I felt the uncontrollable heat start its relentless march up the entire length of my body, immediately suffused in shades of scarlet— one of the pleasant perks of menopause. For the first time all morning, Elizabeth decided she was ready for some bonding time with me. Arrrgh! Even though my inner peace had been heartily challenged throughout the day, I couldn't help but laugh, a healthier response than any of the other available options. It was—just—one of those days.

Call the Doctor

I've always enjoyed my own thoughts, although thinking can be a dangerous pastime, especially if our minds make faulty assumptions or perpetuate grandiose illusions. "For as he thinks within himself, so he is . . ." the writer of Proverbs stated. Scary, but true, I believe. My imagination has transported me into some wonderful—and terrible—adventures and experiences through the years. Most flights of fantasy are delightful trips. Occasionally, a nasty mental journey germinates around the seed of illness, betrayal, fear or death. You know—you "catch" a cold and fear the onset of pneumonia because your co-worker is hospitalized with a case of it; experience sudden pain and fear a heart attack. I used to be much more susceptible to that kind of suggestion and early in our marriage whenever I'd get really sick, I'd check to make sure Cecil's white dress shirt was clean and pressed so he would look presentable at my funeral! I don't spend time worrying about those possibilities anymore, but as I age, I'll likely develop the kind of obsession with my physical self that I began with as a baby.

There is nothing more fascinating when you're a child than your own physical body. Babies and toddlers explore every crack and crevice they have. Life is a mystery, especially when it's new, and we are innately drawn to discovering its intricacies. We are not initially repelled by boogers and doo-doo; puke or pee, either. On the contrary, we are enthralled by their very grossness. It takes several hundred admonishments to "Get that finger out of your nose," before your kids even hear you. They're okay with tasting, too. We have to train those taste buds, often a long, arduous task and one some people never succeed in doing. My cousin, Rodney, once taught us a little ditty that went like this: *Jimmy's always doin' it, pickin' his nose and chewin' it.* You can say, "Ewwwww," to your heart's content but I'd stake my life that we've all sampled that delicacy at some point in our early formative years.

When my grandchildren were toddlers, they frequently enjoyed playing "doctor," with me as their patient. I was not a good patient. I whined and complained, needing constant attention, wanting chicken soup and ginger ale, stories read to me and lullabies sung soothingly. Elizabeth would run tirelessly back and forth to the play kitchen, pretending to cook up a storm, attempting to satisfy my every longing, not merely by being my doctor, but happily "mothering" me, as well.

Daniel and Matthew each had their own approach to doctoring. Daniel, a naturally analytical thinker, first "ordered" tests to assess my specific malady, then, thoughtfully diagnosed my illness as he played my doctor. He looked at me, dead serious, before pronouncing his diagnosis. "It's not good news, Nani," he said, then paused a moment for effect. "It's cancer," he bluntly and matter-of-factly added gloomily. I must admit I was a little disconcerted by his startling dire prognosis.

Collectively, their favorite aspect of this doctor/patient play occurred when I'd unexpectedly start to moan and groan. "I feel a little nauseous. Ohhh. Mmmm. Uhhh. I'm going to throw-up. Hurry, get the bucket." I'd put my best thespian abilities to use and pretend to throw-up, heartily and with gusto, of course, as they stood observing, beaming in sheer delight.

One January morning, shortly after Christmas, three-year-old Matthew and his mother came to visit and help me set up some features on my new computer, a gift from Cecil to me. Well, basically I *watched* as Andrea worked at my computer. Anyway, while she and I were busy at the computer, Matthew was investigating the toys in the family room. Presently, he appeared at his mother's side with an instrument from the play doctor's kit and asked if he could check her ears. She was a compliant patient and he happily peered in her ear. "How do you feel?" he inquired, very professionally.

"I feel fine," she said. Obviously she didn't know how to play this game.

Matthew disagreed. "No. You're sick," he insisted.

"Oh, I am?" she asked. "Do I need some medicine?"

Matthew nodded his head. I told him that I thought I had some medicine and headed for my pantry. I found a small packet of miniature "Sweet Tarts" and emptied them into a little bowl. "Here's some pills you can give your mommy," I told him, handing him the dish.

He briefly and intently studied the tiny colorful balls, looked up at me very seriously and said, "I'm sick, too."

His mommy diplomatically took two pills and told Matthew he could have the rest. This may surprise you but they both made a rapid and complete recovery!

Most of my emergency doctor visits came about because I'm a klutz. I was only about three years old when I poked a bean so far up my nose that my normally unflappable mother, panicked and trotted me to see the doctor. By the time we arrived the bean had begun its descent and required only a pair of tweezers for its safe removal. That event marked my inauspicious introduction to undignified accidents.

When I was a young adult, I cut my thumb washing dishes one Saturday morning. I called my mother who took me to the hospital where I received eight stitches. Naturally I was dressed up for the occasion complete with a head full of giant hair curlers, a face slathered in white cold cream and bright red blood dripping from my hand. (A few years later I'd repeat that escapade—washing dishes, cutting finger, getting stitches.)

I fell multiple times: running to answer the door and tripping over the rug; sliding in the mud, unable to keep my balance as I tried to help my husband move a rock from one place to another in our backyard; at least three times ingloriously falling on the stairs, hurting my backside. The first time that occurred, I was several months pregnant when I carelessly stepped on the top of a long set of wooden steps in my sock feet. My feet went out from under me and I slid down the entire length of stairs, gaining momentum as I went, unable to stop myself, bouncing like a beach ball on every step, laughing and crying at the same time.

I called my mother first. She lived just one street away but was getting ready to go to my sister, Thelma's, for a couple days. "Could you wait a little while before you leave town?" I asked tearfully, explaining what had happened.

I called the doctor, scared to death for my unborn baby. He laughed. "The baby will be okay," he assured me. "It's got lots of padding. Your backside will be sore and get pretty colorful, though," he added cheerfully. He was right. Part of me turned black and blue, pink and purple—and very sore.

If I wasn't falling and injuring a knee or my backside, my personal injury of choice seemed to be to break a toe—five—or six of them. Hmmm. How many? I'm not sure. I have long feet and very long toes. Cecil once facetiously observed that my toes should be equipped with eyeballs or headlights because they get there an hour ahead of the rest of me!

The first time I broke a toe I was barefoot and rammed it into a chair leg. My hubby took me to the emergency room. The doctor taught us standard treatment for a broken toe, that is, tape it to the next toe and wear tight shoes. We had no inkling how valuable that information would be to us in the years ahead. I broke a toe when the wood pile fell over on my foot. That was an especially bad one—but we didn't alter our plans. I taped it to the next toe, put on a pair of pointy toed boots and walked all over New York City the next day with Cecil, our collective five kids and our friends Mike and Rose. That toe never healed correctly but I thoroughly enjoyed seeing various sites such as the Empire State Building and The Museum of Natural History.

A couple of times I broke a toe by not looking where I was going and crashing into the wall or a chair. The last time I broke a toe became a spiritual moment in my history. One summer day, my feet dressed in sandals, I was grocery shopping, accompanied by my then adolescent daughter, Sarah. Pushing the shopping cart, I stopped abruptly for some now forgotten reason, and jammed my little toe full force into the back wheel of the cart. "Uh-oh," I said, "I just broke another toe," looking in dismay at an extremely mangled little appendage. I quickly checked out and hobbled to the car. Once at home, Cecil got an ice pack and we sandwiched that painful, twisted and swollen toe in a frigid nest for a while. This toe was in rough shape and we continued that treatment for a couple hours before attempting to bind it to the adjoining toe because we couldn't completely straighten it. Not only was it swollen, misshapen, and throbbing, it had begun to turn black and blue.

I left the bandage in place for two days. The toe didn't seem to be hurting by the third day and when I removed the bandage I gazed in amazement at a perfectly normal little toe—no swelling, no throbbing, not crooked nor discolored. As I made my bed that morning I mentally celebrated what I knew absolutely to be God's tender healing hands at work—once again. I hadn't asked for healing—shame on me—but God had graciously granted it, regardless. So much of life is comprised of grief and pain—often huge heartaches—but my broken little toe became a big healing blessing to me—not only physically, but emotionally and spiritually, as well. We all periodically wear a pleasant facade, masking an often breaking heart, and I am no exception. With vigilant care and a positive attitude, I believe the body will naturally heal itself—in many cases. I don't know why my little toe received a divine touch this time, except, perhaps, my wounded spirit needed healing, too.

Someone has said that "excuses are like noses, everybody has one and they all smell," or "excuses are like armpits, everybody has two and they both stink." Regular attendance at school was not one of my strengths. I missed a lot of days, always for a good *reason*. I was "sick" whenever my homework wasn't done—every third or fourth day (actually, most every day some piece of homework was likely missing); not having anything to wear made me ill; a test I was unprepared for made me positively nauseous; a bad hair day gave me a headache. Occasionally, I was genuinely sick, of course. Most of those absences my mother graciously accommodated me by supplying a mandatory excuse, e.g., "Please excuse Lela from school on Wednesday because of an upset stomach." Protocol at our school required appearing in front of the school nurse, written excuse in hand, to validate your absence. With a record like mine, I wasn't too popular at the nurse's office. I never really reformed my ways until I became a mother. My girls frequently appeared at my side, thermometer hanging out of their mouths as if it were a cigarette, praying fervently for a fever so I'd let them stay home from school. You're right, girls, it's not fair. Remember that line . . . "Do as I say, not as I do."

When I was about twelve, a big boil called a carbuncle appeared in my armpit. It came with a blessing, though—I was excused from the dreaded gym class for a few days. And I got to see the truly compassionate side of the school nurse. One day during class, when my boil started oozing, I went to the nurse's office—normally the last place I'd choose to visit. Miss McKernan, a fire-breathing tyrant disguised as the school nurse, terrified me. She didn't sugar-coat her words as I meekly tried to explain my problem. "Well, get in here," she said brusquely in total exasperation. "Let me take a look at it." I removed my blouse and lifted my arm. A tiny smile briefly appeared on her face. She said, "You have got quite a boil there, haven't you?" It could have been my over-active imagination, but I'm sure I heard an evil, diabolical laugh echoing in the room. She started to push on both sides of that boil with obvious delight. "Am I hurting you?" she asked with saccharine solicitousness.

It actually didn't hurt too badly but since it was the first time (and the last time) I'd ever been in her good graces, I winced and replied, "Owww. Yes, a little." I couldn't resist dramatizing my pain a bit; it was making her so happy. "Owww," I repeated, grimacing slightly, prolonging her pleasure; she certainly enjoyed playing nurse that day, pushing that nasty old pus out of my boil. It's the *only* time throughout my school years that I can recall her smiling at me. One person's pain may be another's pleasure.

Although I have various minor physical issues that are slightly inconvenient and annoying, other than two successful pregnancies, a pain easily endured and quickly forgotten, I've only ever experienced one major boo-boo. My husband and I were spending the evening at our daughter's house, assisting her oldest son, Sam as he watched his two younger brothers, seven-year-old Daniel and Matthew, who was three. Andrea was taking a class at the local Vo-tech. Matthew is a born rebel and he doesn't care who thinks they're in charge, he knows that's his divinely designated role—to rule the world—or at least his little corner of it. After several minor defiant skirmishes, I picked him up in my arms and stepped over the gate separating the family room from the kitchen/dining area to put him in "time-out." Unfortunately, clumsy me caught one of my big feet on the gate and was instantly forced to choose—drop Matthew or try to shield him as I fell. No choice—save the child. I hit my left side with tremendous impact. Thankfully, Matthew escaped unscathed. I wasn't so lucky. Pain. Giant pain—even for a seasoned martyr like me. I instantly knew my arm was broken. Cecil and Sam both hovered over me ready to assist me as two wide-eyed little boys watched in fear. Grandmothers are not supposed to fall down and go boom. It took a few moments just to gingerly get me up off the floor.

We left three very subdued boys and hurried (Cecil's normal pace, anyway) to the emergency room for a pleasant three hour ordeal. The x-rays showed a broken left arm—actually shoulder. The bone had broken and the lower part had jammed up into the upper part—impacted, the doctor told us. They put my arm in a sling, gave me some pain meds and sent me home to recuperate.

For the first time in my life, I felt totally helpless. I couldn't even pull my pants up or down to pee the first couple of days—my hubby had to do it for me. Although Cecil was very thoughtful, I still felt humiliated and undignified. I couldn't lie down completely for several weeks and had to sleep downstairs in the recliner. The pain was excruciating the first few days and I actually took the pain pills (I am not a fan of drugs and usually refuse them.) Cecil surely earned his halo—finally—it's been a long laborious struggle trying to unobtrusively nudge him into sainthood. He cooked and cleaned and played nurse. And he did a good job.

But he also took over the personal care—you know, the shower, dress and hair routine. I'm not fond of my body in the best of times—picture jiggling jello, or cottage cheese curds. Now picture my strong, aggressive, alpha male heartily scrubbing those jiggling body parts and enthusiastically washing my hair. I lost a little weight and a copious amount of skin cells just getting clean and dry. Cecil has big hands. He's not really the artistic type, adept at fine work, but he tried, he really tired to blow my hair dry—and—style it! After several days of startling myself every time I caught a glimpse of my new hairstyle, I managed to wield the brush with my good arm as he held the blow dryer.

Anyway, we got through it. Cecil made a sample yardstick out of poster board and taped it along side of a doorway and I worked diligently, every day, at the prescribed exercises, forcing my unwilling arm to recover full mobility, always striving to reach a new goal, a higher point on the chart. Even my young grandchildren practiced "walking the wall" with their fingers, just as their Nani was doing. My arm healed completely within a year's time. Once again I am thankful for God's obvious healing hands and the tender care of my husband.

I don't know what the future holds for me on this planet, how long I'll occupy, or what challenges I'll face—physical or otherwise. We tend to live in a state of expectation. Waiting. Always waiting for something more. Perhaps the best is yet to be—if not here, then surely in the next life. I have a direct line to the Great Physician, so I'm not worried. I'm positive that with all the obvious accidents I've had, I've had many more "misses," keeping my angels working overtime. For the most part I've learned to savor the moment, recognizing that yesterday is a memory and tomorrow only a possibility. I'm almost sixty and I've had a pretty good run. I don't want to spend the final chapters of my life story focusing on my health—the problems or the lack thereof. I just want to live, fully engaged, risky as that may be, and then, die—without regrets. I hope to keep "walking the wall" upward, reaching for the goal, the prize that God promises to those who love with all their hearts and minds and souls.

A Thanksgiving Story, 2009

I never recall the school scheduling their teacher conferences the two days prior to Thanksgiving before, but that's how it happened this year, providing my granddaughter, Elizabeth, a golden opportunity to sleep over and help her grandmother [me] get ready for Thanksgiving. I love Thanksgiving. Although Thanksgiving doesn't carry the same spiritual clout of Christmas or Easter, it is, as my friend Sally pointed out, the only holiday unsullied by the secular culture. It is a simple and pure celebration of food, family, memories, and, hopefully, a thankful heart.

This year was our third Thanksgiving without my mother. The first Thanksgiving we celebrated without her was just a few short weeks after her physical departure from the visible world. That year, I made the stuffing—and cried. I peeled potatoes—and cried. I set the table—and cried. While mourning the loss, I knew it was her time to go; her body was worn out. And, I knew, that more than anything Mother would want me to invest myself in the present—in the living—that by doing so, I would honor her best; when you have little people in your world that's not a difficult task. The greatest challenge for me is that as an innate perfectionist, I always want to host a flawless celebration.

Elizabeth arrived about 11:15 on the Tuesday morning before Thanksgiving. Her mother dropped her off and whizzed away, a mere forty-five minutes later than she'd said to expect her—totally normal behavior for Sarah. I greeted a smiling Elizabeth at the door. Still dressed in her pj's and carrying a bag stuffed with miscellaneous items, she announced, "I'm sleeping over." Apparently I didn't know that. Her very next words, emphatically delivered, were, "I'm starving."

"Didn't you have breakfast?" I asked.

"No," she replied. "Mommy slept late and then was on the phone with a client until time to leave."

"Are you sure you didn't eat?" I probe suspiciously. Elizabeth is nine years old and a very capable, self-sufficient young girl—a girl who loves to eat, and freely, liberally, and often covertly, raids my pantry for a variety of snacks.

She vigorously shakes her head. "I didn't," she protests with conviction, looking up at me with eyes wide and guileless. I'm not convinced but I'm her grandmother and she knows it.

"What would you like? Eggs? An English muffin?" There is no response. I yell from the kitchen, "Elizabeth." She doesn't seem to hear me. I call a second time. "Elizabeth?" Elizabeth has dropped her bag by the door, and is already settled in front of the TV, oblivious to the world around her, absolutely certain that her needs will be met. I raise my voice and call once more, "Elizabeth?"

"A toasted English muffin with cream cheese," she replies indifferently, "unless you have a bagel?"

Two toasted muffins and a glass of o.j. later, I firmly remind her that I need to do a grocery store run. "Fifteen more minutes, then the TV must go off and you have to get dressed."

We make a quick stop at the bagel shop before hitting the grocery store. Elizabeth "helps" me at the grocery store. There are four additional items in my shopping cart: an individual gourmet bottle of juice, a bag of Cheetos, a small package of individually wrapped cheese bites, and a can of Chef-Boyardee macaroni & cheese. I'm surprised by the can of mac & cheese. "Are you sure you like this stuff?" I ask incredulously.

"Oh, yes," she assures me. "It's my favorite."

Elizabeth helps me unload; she carries several bags of groceries from the car to the kitchen for me.

She's hungry again. I fix a part of a bagel for her and heat the contents of the can of mac & cheese. "Can you eat the whole can?" I call to her as she is once again ensconced in front of the TV. "Elizabeth? Elizabeth?" I carry her lunch into her and set it on the tray table. I bow obsequiously several times in deference to the queen.

"Nani," she laughingly protests, then scolds me. "You know I don't like you to do that."

I finish unpacking groceries and put them away. I'm occupied with various tasks for a while. The house suddenly gets quiet as the TV is turned off. Elizabeth appears in the kitchen. "I'm ready for my bath now" she tells me.

"Why don't you just take a shower?" I suggest. "It's a lot faster and easier." I'm thinking about my lovely big un-used soaking tub, already occupied by a village of prolifically procreating dust bunnies.

"I want to smell nice for Daniel," she replies. Pop and I and Elizabeth are attending her nine-year old-cousin's concert at his school later that evening. I clean out the tub and pour some pomegranate/mango bath gel under the warm stream of water.

She hops in, prepared to hunker down for a good soak. I'm not comfortable straying far so I wander in and out, watching her having a grand adventure in the land of imagination. Although Elizabeth is a worrier by nature, she momentarily forgets all her worries and fears. She sings and laughs and chatters in sheer pleasure. She washes her own hair. "I need conditioner, too," she affirms. I partially blow dry her beautiful chestnut shoulder-length hair. She stands patiently watching in the mirror as I carefully style it into a smooth, shining bob. While I make admiring comments about her hair, and my handiwork, I watch *her* as she decides to pull it up into a ponytail.

She goes to "her" room to finish dressing and I go downstairs. On my way through the family room, I retrieve the remains of her lunch. The bagel is gone but the bowl of mac & cheese is barely touched. "Why didn't you eat your mac & cheese?" I ask her when she comes downstairs. "I thought it was your favorite."

"It didn't taste good," she said, her mouth grimacing in disgust. She's very expressive. Once again she disappears into the family room and the TV begins to beat its relentless discordant rhythm.

"Elizabeth, you've watched enough TV today," I yell in to her.

"This is my favorite show," she states, ignoring my subtle suggestion.

It seems she has a lot of favorites. I reply, "Okay. But as soon as this show goes off, the TV goes off."

When her favorite show is over, she moves to my computer. I'm busily preparing dinner to a new rhythm; she's brought up a Michael Jackson video and the beat is a bit more frenetic. "Turn the volume down," I yell. I'm the type of person that functions optimally in silence.

After dinner, we join our daughter, Andrea, and her two youngest boys, Daniel and Matthew, for Daniel's entertaining concert. To celebrate Daniel's moment, we share an ice cream cake at Andrea's afterwards, then hurry home. It is the grand finale of the only TV show I've watched religiously all season— *Dancing with the Stars*. Elizabeth gets into her jammies, brushes her teeth and settles enthusiastically next to me on the loveseat. She's excited to stay up late and she, too, loves this show. By 9:30, her head in my lap, she is sound asleep. My hubby is snoring in his recliner on my other side. I sit between them, frozen in place for the next hour and a half, watching the show all by myself.

Elizabeth is not yet comfortable sleeping alone at our house. When I had asked her earlier if she was going to sleep by herself, she'd replied, "I'm thinking about it." She thought me right into bed with her. My house is a big ole structure that creaks and groans heartily and she hears every eerie sound it makes—plus a few. I remember what those kinds of fears feel like.

I didn't plan to do anything but prepare for Thanksgiving dinner the next day. Elizabeth moved between the TV and my computer and kept the beat going. "Call me when you're ready to do the pies," she hollers out to me.

When the crust is ready, I call her to come and mix the ingredients for pumpkin pie. She loves to bake. And sample. She gets a spoon and digs every smidgen of pie dough out of the bowl, licking her lips as if it were some gourmet delicacy. Just as I'm gingerly placing the pies in the oven, the phone rings. "Can you answer it for me, Elizabeth?" I ask. It is the Stroudsburg School asking me to pick up my great-niece, Breanna, who is in the nurse's office. Her dad cannot be reached on his cell and I'm an emergency contact person for his two children. I've not showered and I just put two pies in the oven.

I call Andrea and ask to drop off Elizabeth so I don't expose her to potentially hazardous bugs—it *is* the year of the notorious swine flu—then rush through the shower. I'm ready to go, pacing the floor, watching the timer. The deep dish pie is not done. I worry aloud, "It's taking forever. What am I going to do?"

"Why don't you just turn the oven off and leave the pie in?" suggests my very bright granddaughter.

"Good idea. Why didn't I think of that?" I reply and we hurry out the door.

As I'm running from Andrea's door to my car, I turn my ankle and simultaneously feel a snap in my right foot. "Oh, Lela," I mutter, hobbling in pain to the car. Tears of frustration sting my eyes but I don't have time to wallow. Breanna is waiting in the nurse's office and her face lights up when she sees me. She's disappointed to discover that she is not coming to my house to play with Elizabeth—they're only four months apart in age—but I can't risk exposure and I deliver her to her grandmother, my sister Thelma.

I retrieve Elizabeth and we head home. I take a perfectly done pie out of the oven, grab an ice pack from the freezer and sit with my foot up. "Would you run upstairs and look in Pop's drawer next to his sink for an ace bandage?" I ask my solicitous nurse. I wrap my arch and ankle snuggly.

"Elizabeth, would you bring me the phone?" I call the church to tell them I won't make the prayer group I normally attend. I call my hubby. Andrea and Sam had already taken care of that task. He's about ready to head home but he's two hours south and it is a nasty, drizzly day.

I have things to do and a substantial "martyr complex" to nurture—that "I'll do it myself, thank you very much" mentality. Even though the beat is once again beating away, I ask "Would you run up and get Grandma's old cane for me?" Her young legs scurry to comply. Between ice pack applications, I periodically get up and tackle several small tasks. I make a comprehensive list of food preparations in the order they need to be addressed. Elizabeth watches me hobbling around, using Great-Grandma's cane. "I don't like to see you like this," she says with obvious distress. Grandmothers are supposed to be immutable and indestructible.

Thanksgiving morning I sauté the onions and celery Cecil had chopped the previous evening, and prepare the stuffing. Cecil stuffs the bird and puts it in the oven. He peels the potatoes. I cringe silently as half the potato goes with the peel. He washes and chunks the sweet potatoes and puts them over to boil. I sit at the counter giving directions as diplomatically as possible. He doesn't take orders very well and gets a little testy as I'm guiding him through the process of making the sweet potato soufflé. "Who's the boss here?" I firmly ask. My infirmity has made me brave. You don't hit a guy when he's down—even if you want to.

The kids arrive. Sarah and Elizabeth are actually early—a true miracle—and, she baked cranberry bread for our feast. Andrea's family arrives, bringing a green bean casserole and the enthusiasm of three hungry boys. I make a feeble attempt to "hallow" the moment. "After dinner we'll each tell one thing we're thankful for." Dream on, Lela. By the time the meal is over, conversation has deteriorated into an argument over whether or not our revered Native American ancestors regularly smoked pot. My blood pressure rises as I am outnumbered in my opinion that they did not. Lethargy grips us all as we are too full to even consider dessert. The telephone rings. Sarah answers. It is my sister Clara. Sharp-tongued Sarah regales her aunt with a colorful, embellished rendition of her mother's [me] infirmity, amusing most of the listeners on this end—except me—I'm having a bit of a personal pity party.

As Sarah is enjoying the moment, she inexplicably finds herself sitting on her butt—ON THE FLOOR!! She is laughing helplessly but she has no idea how she went from standing still to this humble position. We all instantly think—Grandma!! Whenever Sarah would get smart-mouthed with me, Grandma would swat her and say, "Now, Sarah." Sarah is not physically hurt but, perhaps, appropriately chastised? Even *my* morose mood lightened as I thought of Mother participating in our Thanksgiving celebration. Her good sense of humor appears to have transcended realities.

I miss my mother immensely; she was a positive integral part of our daily lives for so many years. Yet, I celebrate those who are living. I am often frustrated or amused by those in my life; challenged or comforted; wounded or healed; but, most of all, I love wholeheartedly, thankful that I am loved in return.

I wanted perfection – I got LIFE. Life is not meant to be a smooth perfect path from one end to the other. The pot-holes to navigate, the mountains to climb and rivers to cross are meant to help build our inner muscles—spiritual, relational muscles. When we arrive at the other end, our bodies may be battered, bruised and broken by the journey, but, if we cede control of our lives to God, our spirits will flourish and sprout wings— wings strong enough to lift us upward, when the time is right, to a Thanksgiving banquet where we will join hands together in perfect harmony.

In spite of my injury, I truly enjoyed Thanksgiving. Still, at the end of the day, when everyone had gone to their respective homes and Cecil had gone up to bed, I sat in my rocker by the fire and cried like a baby.

Fatal Fragrance

Staying up late had become habitual. Between menopause, and grief over the recent death of my beloved mother, I often found insomnia my nighttime companion, besides my husband that is. This night was no different. I climbed into bed shortly after 11 p.m., then laid wide awake, listening to my husband's erratic snoring and the endless chatter of my mind, trying to convince my brain that I was okay and it could shut down the system for the night. I placed two fingers gently against the pulse on my right wrist. Thud-thud, thud-thud, thud-thud. Pause. Thud-thud, thud-thud, thud-thud, thud-thud. Pause. Andrea was right. I did have an irregular heartbeat. I was pretty sure of it anyway. I'd had a follow-up visit at the doctor's a few days earlier and the nurse in the doctor's office initially thought my heart was beating irregularly, then did a cursory second check and decided she was mistaken. Yesterday, while visiting my daughter, she checked my pulse and blood pressure and definitely felt an irregular beat.

I did some self-talk, trying to convince my run-a-way imagination that I was not facing imminent death. I've had a little leak in my mitral valve all my life and never suffered any serious repercussions. But, I am getting older and I had recently experienced a nasty fall, breaking my left shoulder and going into shock in the process. My heart could be starting to weaken.

I rolled on my side, finally feeling the first subtle symptoms of sleep, when a powerful sweet fragrance wafted under my nose. Instantly alert, I lifted my head to sniff the air. The smell evaporated. Having had some paranormal experiences in the past, often involving illusory aromas, I immediately began analyzing the significance of the odor, who it represented, and, most importantly, who it was beckoning to, that is, inviting to come to the other side. My first thought—me, of course. I started to pray. I negotiated with God for a little more time—at least until there was more peace and order, less discord and chaos in the lives of my children, and my grandchildren were all a bit older. I softly mentioned everyone I care about by name, quietly pleading for their health and safety. And, I prayed fervently, with all my heart for myself.

I checked my pulse again. Thud-thud, thud-thud, thud-thud. Pause. Thud-thud, thud-thud, thud-thud-thud-thud. Pause. I rolled over on my back. Once again that same sweet fragrance floated under my nose. Well . . . so be it. I'm at peace with myself, with God, and with those I care most about.

I must have disturbed my sleeping hubby, because he sat up and headed for the bathroom to pee. "It's good that he's awake," I thought. "I can say my loving farewells to him, remind him of my funeral and burial wishes, and give him some other final instructions." When he climbed back in bed, I noticed a slight fragrance. I stuck my nose next to him and sniffed. He smelled awfully sweet. "Did you put lotion on before you got in bed tonight?" I asked.

"Yeah," he replied. "I used some old stuff that I found in the cabinet."Although it's not unusual for him to lotion his dry arms and legs, he normally applies a fragrance-free lotion. He smelled like a flower tonight. The same sweet smell I'd been dying over for the past hour.

It's truly amazing but my heart beat instantly appeared to assume a normal rhythm. I silently chuckled, rolled back on my side, closed my eyes and slept peacefully the rest of the night. All that worrying for nothing. As my beloved grandmother would have said, "The cloud I feared with dread, broke with mercy on my head." *Who of you by worrying can add a single hour to your life . . . therefore do not worry about tomorrow, for tomorrow will worry about itself. Each day has enough trouble of its own* (Matt. 6:27, 34).

Insulin and Angels

We were planning a trip to Hawaii to visit my eldest sister, Jennie, and wanted to take my mother along with us. We had recently moved her from an hour north of us to a little house a couple miles away because she appeared to be physically declining and needed more vigilant and attentive care. Since she had gained weight and gotten very lethargic, even sluggish, which we ignorantly attributed to aging, I tried to sign her up for a senior citizen exercise program at the local hospital to ensure she'd be able to enjoy this once-in-a-lifetime trip to a faraway, tropical paradise. They wisely demanded she see a doctor for a physical, first. We hadn't lived in the area long, and although I had a pediatrician for the kids, we did not yet have a family doctor. I called a recently opened local medical office to make an appointment. Some people might see it as chance, or perhaps fortuitous, but I truly believe it was providential. They set an appointment for her with a young doctor; a doctor who would become an integral part of her life over the next twenty years, and one we would come to respect and love. Within minutes, Dr. Foster realized her thyroid was not functioning. "In six months you won't recognize her," he told me as he began the process of readjusting her system via prescribed drugs, initially for diabetes and thyroid. Since he also found some other potentially life-threatening issues, we added an apartment on the rear of our home for her, where Mother would live for the next twenty years until her death at the age of almost ninety-two. Before her sojourn in this dimension ended, she would be on a daily regimen of a dozen or more drugs, and fight a constant, and ultimately losing battle, to keep her system working efficiently. In the last few years of her life, my ailing mother became insulin dependent. Twice every day, before both breakfast and dinner, I would check her blood glucose on a meter and then administer her insulin, a process neither of us enjoyed but faithfully adhered to as directed by the doctor.

One day when I was babysitting five-year-old Elizabeth, she and I went next door when it was time for the late afternoon routine and Elizabeth sat down opposite my mother at her kitchen table. She winced when I stuck Great-Grandma's finger to obtain a tiny drop of blood to check her sugar level. As I began preparing the needle, a visibly distressed Elizabeth said, "I can't look," and hid her face in her arms. "I hate needles," she added vehemently. A split second later she urgently yelled, "Wait. Don't give Grandma her needle, yet." I paused in my task. "Can I have a piece of paper?" she asked.

"What are you doing?" I queried curiously, proceeding to continue preparing the needle. "You better hurry," I urged her. "I can't wait too long. Grandma has to have her insulin on time."

Elizabeth quickly plied pen to paper, hurrying to complete some mysterious yet critical task. She thrust the paper in front of her Great- Grandma Gillow, sighed in relief and said, "There. I drew a picture of an angel for Grandma to look at so the needle won't hurt." Who could experience pain with a picture like that placed in front of them, thoughtfully created by an empathetic, loving little person?

Usually, whenever I was babysitting for my grandchildren, Mother would come over to my house and sit in the family room, just to enjoy the little people. She didn't really play with them; she merely provided a consistent warm, secure presence for them. Everyone benefited. I could perform short tasks in the kitchen without worry, making her feel useful, which she was, and she received emotional nourishment as the recipient of the little people's constant need for attention. Likewise, the little people felt loved and safe. If they were disobedient or misbehaved a bit, I'd threaten them with my wooden spoon, pretending to be angry by turning into the "Nani Monster." We all knew it was a game and one which we all enjoyed playing. I designated Great-Grandma as "gold." That meant that for whatever the reason, they could run to her for refuge, and the "Nani Monster" couldn't touch them. Both Mother and the little person she was embracing at the moment would beam happily—an aura of sunshine encompassing them as if they were angels wearing shimmering gold halos.

One day, when I was babysitting for Elizabeth, who was about three years old at the time, Mother and I were sitting in the family room watching her play. The door connecting Mother's apartment to our house opened into our family room and Mother had left it ajar so she could hear her telephone more readily. Elizabeth seized the opportunity—an open door does seem like an invitation—and quickly ran over to Grandmas' and then back through the family room, disappearing into my front room, which I call my "sanctuary." She was carrying Grandma's cane, an object Mother had begun to utilize on occasion and one that was strictly off limits to the little people.

"Elizabeth," I called from the family room. "What are you doing in there?"

"I'm praying to Jesus," she promptly replied.

"Good answer," I thought, sharing an amused look with my mother. Elizabeth had deliberately taken a taboo object, ran into my Sanctuary, and told me she was praying. Only three and already adeptly practicing adult machinations. I bit. "What are you praying about?"

"I'm praying that you won't be mad at me for taking Grandma's cane," she answered. For some reason she didn't sound even a little frightened of that possibility! She was confident and secure in the love of her people.

The dynamics of our home environment changed drastically after my beloved mother went home to be with Jesus. Even when the sun was shining, it lacked warmth or cheer; much of the time a vast, dark, cold emptiness filled our space. One day in January, a few months after Mother's passing, I was babysitting once again, this time for Matthew, who was three years old at the time. I always teased my mother that she loved her boys best, although I know it wasn't true. But she did "light up" when one of those boys—sons, (or sons-in-law), grandsons or great-grandsons—came in the room. "Well, Dan, or John, Cecil, or Bob," she would say with pleasure. In his beautiful eulogy for her, our pastor friend, Dan Hall, mentioned ". . . it was the way she said your name. . ." You knew when she greeted you that you were special to her—both genders inclusively. She always asserted that the boys were easier than the girls—not as temperamental, in her opinion. Matthew had spent enough time at our house to remember those warm, comforting moments with Great-Grandma.

Even though the day was tinged with sadness, Matthew and I had a wonderful time together on that first, long solo babysitting experience. I missed Mother sitting in her spot, smiling in pleasure at the joy of a little person's play. Matthew seemed to be content, apparently not noticing anything different; he just enjoyed playing. After Matthew went home, however, I suddenly found myself sobbing at the huge loss of goodness in my world, remembering Mother on one of those kinds of days—coming over, sitting on the loveseat, covering her lap with an afghan—being completely and happily "present" in the moment.

Grandma was always on our minds and we spoke of her and our grief frequently. A few days after Matthew had spent the day with me, he suddenly blurted out to his mother, "Grandma's not always in heaven. Sometimes she's at Nani's house."

"How do you know?" his mother asked in surprise, her body on full alert. We are so curious about the unseen world, and, if we're smart, we pay close attention to the little people's insights and observations since they seem to have 20/20 vision into the world that's invisible to the rest of us.

"She talks to me," he stated matter-of-factly.

"Oh? What does she say?"

"She says, 'Hi, Matthew. I love you,'" he replied, the inflection in his words mimicking my mother's.

"Did you see her?" Andrea asked in fascination.

"Yes," he nonchalantly said. "She was sitting in the chair under the window."

Matthew had the words right and the place, too. Mother had been gone about four months but I believe he knew and was secure in the warm reality of her presence. I believe and I am comforted.

Elizabeth drew an angel for Great-Grandma to look at so she wouldn't feel any pain when she got her needle. Matthew, who hadn't been at our home, by himself, for such a long stretch of time (six hours), saw Great-Grandma and played contentedly for hours. Life's stresses can be diminished if we look, and actually see, as the little people so readily do, the transcendent, ubiquitous love surrounding us.

I desperately need some new glasses.

Same Size Next Year

Weight was never a problem for me as an adolescent or teenager. I grew tall and thin, or as one of my sister's boyfriends matter-of-factly stated while giving me a critical once over, "you're really long and linky." I ate whatever I wanted without gaining weight. Somewhere in my mid-twenties I realized that I was beginning to lose that ability as pounds began insidiously creeping on and I found myself embroiled in a lifelong feud between two natural enemies—eating versus maintaining a healthy weight.

It was not as if I were blatantly attacking an evil enemy. Everybody knows you have to eat to live. But, my taste buds unerringly honed in on specific foods—you know the ones—they taste really good but immediately attach themselves to their favorite landing sites—hips, thighs, and tummies. These are not transient visitors, though, coming for a one-night sleepover. Nope. This looks like home to them and they come prepared to stay, carrying heavy suitcases. They put on their sweatpants, a baggy t-shirt and their old bedroom slippers, settle in on the couch, pick up the remote control and a big bag of chips—with sour cream and onion dip, of course—and proceed to doze off, where they remain—comfortable and content forever. I'm still wearing candy, cookies, cakes and pies from forty years ago. Although I never got obese, my weight fluctuated for years, enough that I needed a new wardrobe as I periodically gained and lost ten or fifteen pounds. I kept my old clothes, though, just in case. I finally leveled off in my late forties and stuck there—about twenty-five pounds over a healthy, normal weight for my height and age.

Only one time over the years did I actually go on a real diet—and successfully lose those twenty-five pounds. I kept the weight off for a couple of years before adding it all back, plus a little. Many times I'd attempt to alter my eating habits and I'd lose five pounds, and then promptly gain it back. My intentions were good but my self-control was entirely subject to my present emotional health. If my husband got mad at me, I'd eat a candy bar for comfort. If the kids were suffering in a difficult relationship, or behaving rebelliously, I'd eat a piece of cake. If there wasn't enough money or time, or if my feelings were hurt, or . . . whatever the reason, I'd make a batch of cookies and eat a couple. I rarely over-ate; I just ate the wrong food at the wrong time for the wrong reasons. There is nothing much more comforting when you feel distressed than food— that's why they call it "comfort food," I guess. It temporarily appears to ease the pain slightly, until you step on the scales, look in the mirror, or try to squeeze into a pair of snug jeans, that is.

My hubby frequently went on hunting trips through the years—usually he'd be gone ten days to two weeks. Almost without fail, I'd resolve to redeem that time by losing a few pounds, hoping to razzle-dazzle him when he returned. Once when he went away, I determined that this was the time—I was going to do it. I made a big pot of turkey soup. My slender hairdresser had told me that's how she'd lost weight—she ate lots of soup. I ate soup. I ate lots of soup, and a little salad. What an exemplary model of discipline and self-control I'd become. Then, feeling lonely, deprived and in serious need of comfort, I made a big pan of double-fudge brownies which I proceeded to carefully ration over the last few days my husband was away. I was definitely going to lose some weight, but it's a well-documented fact that it's not wise to deprive yourself too stringently.

I waited until the afternoon of my hubby's return, almost the very last minute, before checking my success. I had showered, shaved my legs and underarms, and trimmed my fingernails and toenails early that morning. First I peed, squeezing out every drop I could, peeled off all my clothes, including my eyeglasses and got on the scales. "What? How can this possibly be correct," I wondered. The scales indicated that I'd gained two pounds. It couldn't be right. No way. Absolutely not. "It's these cheap, inaccurate scales," I thought. "They're nothing but worthless trash." Irate, I stepped off and pushed those scales around with my foot. They probably just needed a little adjustment or weren't positioned properly. I removed my watch, then, my earrings. The only thing I was left wearing was my wedding ring. I climbed back on. Three pounds? "Impossible!" I yelled in disbelief. Perplexed by this amazing phenomenon, I thought to myself, "That's some heavy wedding ring you've got there, Lela."

I've learned to be content as I am—it's much less stressful. And I don't have to eat for comfort any more—although I do occasionally. It's so—well—comforting.

The Joy of Working
with Cecil

Some people are born industrious; others are innately self-disciplined and some people are highly motivated achievers. I'm an ambitious dreamer. I effortlessly imagine myself trim and fit—from the comfort of my easy chair, and I can clearly picture myself signing my international bestseller in my bedtime fantasies. My house is immaculate, my meals gourmet masterpieces, and my wisdom revered—all from the fertile ground of imagination. Basically, I nibble at work and feast on dreams. I'm not exactly lazy; I merely prefer investing my energy in emotional, spiritual and relational work—and it *is* work—than in the visual, tangible dimension of life. Occasionally I do work up a sweat doing serious cleaning or cooking or weeding in the flower garden. Usually, however, I try to straighten up, pick up, and put away right behind the activity. It saves a lot of energy that way. I believe in saving energy.

Both my mother and father, as products of the rural farming community they grew up in, wholeheartedly embraced the "Protestant work ethic." Although my father died when I was a child, I was privileged to observe my mother's natural industry as she lived into her early nineties. She always seemed to love to work; her hands were rarely idle. In retrospect, though, she did enjoy some tasks much more than others. She loved to create: sewing nightwear for various offspring; crocheting doilies, baby afghans and edges on pillow cases and/or towels; writing cards and notes to various friends and family, and she heartily enjoyed all aspects of edibles, from the inception—planting, harvesting, preserving, cooking, baking, to the finish—the pleasure of eating. And she loved to clean windows and wash dishes. Oh, yes, and re-arrange the furniture, a trait that she said annoyed my dad to no end. "My mother never moved the furniture," she'd acerbically mimic him saying.

During my adolescent and teenage years, five of us were crammed into a mobile home that even with the addition of a room on the back still made for tight living quarters. With too much stuff and too many people, we should have worked harder at orderliness, but instead lived surrounded by cheerful disarray. Mother justifiably expected her children to be responsible, but as a widow and sole provider, she didn't have the energy to enforce those expectations. My sister, Clara, and I took a lot of long walks and read a lot of books. Once in a great while we cleaned our bedroom. We might have dried the dishes, too. I'm not very proud of my early work ethics.

Then I got married.

Cecil is an alpha male, one of those men who innately believe they were put on the earth to rule. He is the most driven man I've ever known. He works hard. He works a lot. He works fast. He does not enjoy working.

Shortly after we got married, we decided to dress up our kitchen. We didn't have the financial resources to do major remodeling so we merely wallpapered the room—walls and the challenging ten foot high ceiling. It was the first job we worked at together. It's a real adrenalin rush for most of us ladies to redecorate our homes. I was happily humming that morning, cheerfully watching my highly proficient handyman measuring the dimensions of the walls and ceiling, naively prepared to be his ace assistant should he so need me to be. I'm not above taking orders in areas I know little about. Where I really excel, of course, is in spectator work—and—I'm an enthusiastic encourager.

"I love this yellow wallpaper," I gushed effusively. "Don't you love this wallpaper? It's going to brighten up this whole room. I'll have to get new curtains for the window, though," I added thoughtfully.

"Uhh," he grunted.

"We'll probably have to paint the cabinets, too; they look a little dingy." I was pacing around the room, studying it with a critical eye. "Well, would you look at this? I never noticed how worn the floor is over here. Do you see this? Look, Cecil. Look how shabby this floor is. It's worn in several places. I think we're going to need to replace the linoleum. What do you think?"

"Hmmm," he muttered, busily prepping for the task at hand.

While I watched, cheerfully chattering away, Cecil measured the first piece of wallpaper, cut it, dampened it, carried it over to the corner and stepped onto the ladder. What a great job we were doing. This was going to be fun.

"Are you just going to stand there yapping all day?" he practically spit at me. I stared at him in amazement. Now what could have triggered that reaction? "Well, are you going to help or not?" he bellowed, glaring down at me.

"I'm sorry. What do you want me to do?" I meekly replied, surprised by this unexpected sharp reprimand.

"I need you to guide the paper and make sure it's touching my mark, if it's not too much trouble, that is," he snarled at me sarcastically, visibly annoyed.

I'm looking for his mark; there are several marks in the general area. Looking. Looking. Looking.

Exasperated, he yells, "Anytime today."

"I think I've got it." Carefully I guide the paper to his mark.

"It's got to go left a little. Pull it out." I begin gently loosening the paper. I'm not fast enough. He gives it a jerk and it rips slightly. "Great. Just great. Look what you made me do. We're going to use it anyway. Let's start again, if you think you can follow directions." He doesn't mind little mistakes that are my fault. He positions the paper once more. "To the left," he orders.

I'm trying to obey orders. I carefully move it to the right.

"Are you deaf? I said left," he shouted.

Which is my left, I wonder. My brain is paralyzed. I move it very gingerly to the left.

"Too much. Too much," Cecil yells loudly. "Do I have to do everything myself?"

Tears sting my eyes and we've only just begun the project.

Before the job was done I had learned how to successfully work with Cecil. Very simple rules to follow. First, and most importantly, don't talk—at all. Speak only when commanded. "Woof. Woof." It is absolutely imperative that you are a Cecil psychic; you must be able to read his mind. This is to ensure that whatever he wants—needs spoken, or unspoken—are instantly and smoothly granted or executed before he himself even knows what it is he wants. Finally, you must keep a sweet and peaceful demeanor throughout. It's a little like receiving a spanking and then being told you can't cry. The only person allowed to be annoyed and visibly express it, is Cecil. He's the boss, after all.

I learned the rules the hard way and vowed that I would never, **not ever** get myself into any of those potentially precarious positions in the future.

Three years later, Cecil opened a new company an hour south of our home. I must have forgotten my vow because I miraculously found myself sitting at a desk in a small office as Cecil's secretary. Working in the office offered new challenges. The stakes were the same, the emotional health and ultimate survival of our marriage, but the material consequences were much more hazardous. Ruin a piece of wallpaper in your own house and the repair is a few tears and little dollars; mess up paperwork on a new home contract or say the wrong thing and you could be looking at boodle bucks down the drain.

Did I mention my only business skills were a year of typing in high school, good penmanship, a polite and pleasant phone voice, keeping the office neat and tidy, and a consistently level personality? The phone was a bit of a challenge—it had two lines. I'm not a good multi-tasker. I had a little trouble lying, too. "If you want me to say you're not here, then leave," I courageously informed him. Some husbands and wives work well together, so I've been told, but we were off to an inauspicious start and the future did not look promising.

Since we needed to establish credit, we had to pay cash for everything in the beginning. Cecil was eking out a small profit building several homes that had been sold by a company now in bankruptcy. Every delivery required a check on the spot. Sometimes Cecil would have to take the large cumbersome checkbook with him when he needed to make several stops at supply houses or township buildings.

One day he headed out the door to address various business matters, including dropping off a check at the local glass company. Our office was located in the basement/garage of a real estate office right off the interstate, in a highly visible location. Cecil had repeatedly heard that the mantra for a good business is, "location, location, location" and had approached the owners of the building with an offer too good to refuse— he'd renovate the basement and pay them rent to boot. To combat the dark interior, he'd replaced the garage door with a double sliding glass door. About five minutes after he'd left on this day, I realized he'd forgotten the checkbook, placed strategically visible on the corner of my desk—so we wouldn't forget it, of course. I groaned inside. I was in deep doo-doo. Cell phones were several years in the future. I'd just have to wait it out.

In no time at all, Cecil came careening back in the drive, tires squealing in protest. I hadn't seen him yet, but I knew he'd be fuming and in a big hurry. Everything is urgent to Cecil and his stock answer to the question, "When do you need this?" is always, "Yesterday." He's always in a rush. How could I redeem myself? Could I redeem myself? Experience said "Nope." So I bravely grabbed the checkbook, opened the slider a mere crack as he strode to the door, a fierce scowl darkening his countenance, placed the checkbook in his outstretched hand, quickly slid the door shut and locked it. We momentarily stood there facing each other from opposite sides of the glass door, he energetically yelling at me for my lack of efficiency. But I'm pretty brave from the other side of a locked door; all the while he's yelling at me, I'm standing there smiling at him—and waving; smiling—and waving; smiling—and waving. I amused myself. I don't know why he didn't think it was funny.

I need to amuse myself frequently. A sense of humor has helped me survive many otherwise lost causes. I usually try to lighten the mood when it sinks oppressively, as if into a hot, humid summer day when the air is too thick and heavy for an easy breath and you feel as if you're about to suffocate. During my brief work alliance with Cecil, I'd occasionally wait until he couldn't respond, when he was on the phone with a customer, for instance, and I'd place a highly suggestive risqué message on his desk, or a wonderfully eloquent letter of resignation. I resigned several times before eventually making it a permanent move.

Sometime later, when his business was thriving and he had an impressive work force to intimidate, besides the necessary tasks to keep a household running smoothly, I focused my energies in relational activities: raising kids, taking care of my mother, and working in the church. By default, at one point, I found myself as director of women's ministries at our church.

Among the various facets of the ministry, we periodically held a "work day" where we might make crafts to sell at the annual convention, the proceeds to benefit the missionary supply closet, or fashion small crafts to distribute to residents in a local nursing home. Much of our time on work days, however, was spent "rolling bandages." Worn sheets, donated by various members of the congregation, were washed and bleached, ripped into strips, sewn together into longer strips and delivered to our ladies to roll for bandages. The finished product was then packed into boxes and shipped overseas to missionary hospitals.

Usually, work days brought out the older ladies—the ladies who actually liked rolling bandages—a tedious task from my perspective as the young leader (late thirties.) I'd bring some peppy Christian music to lighten the atmosphere and we'd all bring a bag lunch, then proceed to spend our day enjoying the companionship of fellow sojourners.

I'm telling you all this so you'll grasp how my hubby truly views work.

One day, about ten ladies were gathered for a work day, most of them in their sixties, seventies and eighties. I loved these dear gentle ladies, ladies who reminded me of my beloved grandmother, several of them dressed in print housedresses, gray hair pulled up in buns. We were all set up, having a grand old time cheerfully rolling bandages when the rooster strutted into the henhouse, that is, Cecil surprised me by stopping in for a moment. Cecil is the kind of guy who teases the ladies and makes them all feel special. Many of them were widows and they were delighted to get some masculine attention. Still, these ladies were die-hard workers, so even with a major attractive distraction, they steadily plugged away at the task. Cecil watched for a few moments, fascinated by our industry. Then he felt compelled to give us a bit of guidance from his vast work experience. Isn't *that* a surprise?

"Let me just show you one little thing," he offered generously. He took an unrolled strip of sheet, wrapped it around a pencil, and proceeded to show us how fast we could roll those bandages with this simple little tool. We all dutifully watched his demonstration, oohing and aahing over the speed with which he rolled that bandage. "You'll get the job done a lot faster if you implement this method," he wisely informed us. How about that—a seminar in how to efficiently and expeditiously roll bandages—free of charge, to boot!

Cecil couldn't linger, of course, he was a busy man with things to do and places to go—and in a hurry, too—always.

We picked up right where we'd left off—minus pencils, though. You see, the job wasn't about speed—or even efficiency, although I believe in giving my best to any task. The job was more about the priceless, fleeting moment in time, about camaraderie and relationship, than it was about tangible results. Still, I'm pleased to report, at the end of the day we had an impressive pile of rolled bandages to send off to a hospital in South Africa.

A few years later, when we built our current home, we wallpapered the entire large house—every room. By this time his building business was prospering, and he had many offers for assistance from supposed "expert" wallpaper hangers. He agreed to let a couple of them help but he quickly discovered that none of them met his demanding criteria for the job. You see, they didn't know those critical rules for working with Cecil. And they didn't love him; not as I loved him, that is. Only I qualified for the job. We worked together like a pair of synchronized swimmers—smoothly and efficiently, and silently, of course.

To an alpha human judging work as effort expended in tangible labor, relationship may not correlate with his or her picture of authentic work. But relationships *are* work—likely the hardest work we'll ever do in our lives—and, I believe, the most important. It takes a lot of authentic love to emotionally survive the high stress of the job—love that requires a conscious commitment to another, in spite of innate pettiness, volatile personalities, fragile egos, or betrayal of trust. You can't get the job done fast, either. And there is no retirement date. It's a lifetime career.

Cecil and I tackled a few other major projects over the years—re-modeling two bathrooms and the master bedroom, among others. The finished product is beautiful and personally satisfying, although the elbow grease required never evolved into pleasure for Cecil. I think he still hears his father's merciless criticism reverberating in his ear—a father he could never please. Although Cecil never discovered joy in work, he did eventually learn to laugh at himself and a spoonful of laughter lightens the load considerably.

All the copious amounts of blood, sweat and tears that go into the job remain invisible. Those battle wounds, like so many inflicted over the span of numerous years in relationship, are an integral part of the portrait of our lives. The splashes of red blood of heartache and pain, blue raindrop tears of grief and sadness, and the anger, frustration and fear of black storm clouds provide balance and texture in an otherwise uninspiring, bland landscape. When combined with the bright, sunny yellow moments of laughter, the rainbows of hope and promise, the still, peaceful verdant waters of rest and nourishment, the portrait is complete—a work of art—a true masterpiece called relationship or marriage and, perhaps, even, life.

I've learned some constructive lessons from my years with Cecil: I talk less—a lot less; I delay pleasure until my work is done; I see possibilities rather than obstacles; I learned to look ahead to the next step or need, and, the really big one—the "fanny flag" indicating a slow-moving vehicle disappeared from my generous behind! (I knew if I looked hard enough, I'd find redemption for those scary moments of working with Cecil.)

"Whatever you do, work at it with all your heart, as working for the Lord, not for men . . ." (Col. 3:23). That I can do—I try to do—I will do—with all my heart.

Sally and the Sheep

All marriages have their ups and downs and even though we were going away to celebrate our anniversary, it was not an "up" time in our marriage. A young couple had insidiously insinuated their way into our lives, a couple we initially socialized with regularly—inviting them to dinner at our house, or taking them and their children out to eat. My husband's business was thriving at the time and besides financial resources, we were also investing a lot of time and energy in them. Before long they apparently felt no compunction about receiving help and by sharing their sad story with my generous husband, who has a hard time saying "no" to sad stories, they convinced him to build them a home—to their specifications— where they would live without any financial obligation for two years, at which time they would secure a mortgage and repay Cecil's magnanimous largesse. Lucille, a bold, in-your-face kind of woman, used her feminine wiles to emotionally seduce my husband and a chasm opened wide between us—me, that is, and both my husband and them.

A few weeks before our little trip, I bravely, but with fear and trepidation, broached this uncomfortable situation and requested that my husband secure our investment. He wasn't happy about it, but he did comply, finally drawing up the paperwork that would ensure the house would revert to us should they be unable to acquire a mortgage. He made sure it was signed by them, notarized and recorded just before we left.

The atmosphere was tense as we headed north. Cecil has two speeds—fast—and faster. He has a difficult time relaxing. So we sat silently, listening to the tires humming as we tried to set a new record between our corner of northeastern Pennsylvania and Maine, our get-a-way destination. We didn't even try to pretend we were enjoying ourselves. We were keeping a tradition by taking a short trip for our anniversary, celebrating twenty some odd years of wedded bliss, but we both knew that there was no "bliss" in our union at the moment.

Several times I had tried, unsuccessfully, to convince Cecil we needed reservations. He likes to wing it. But cautious me decided to make one more attempt. "Shouldn't we try and call ahead for reservations?" I asked tentatively, my triple A travel guide in hand.

"Nah," he kinda growled. "You worry too much. They'll be lots of rooms," he added confidently.

"But it is the beginning of the prime travel season," I gently protested. "We should at least see what's available."

"What part of no don't you understand?" he retorted, his ire blatantly obvious.

"I'm sorry." I could hear the saccharine sweetness in my voice as I meekly tried to placate my volatile husband and avert a trek into dangerous territory. I say "I'm sorry" a lot. I desperately wanted to redeem the vested energy and find some marital peace, though, so I shut my mouth and began silently talking to God instead. We traveled quietly for several hours, finally stopping to pee, gas up, and drive-thru McDonald's for a milkshake, the tension easing slightly as the miles piled up.

We arrived in Portland, Maine early evening and stopped at a motel to check in—except—they were booked full. After the third stop, the concierge took pity on us and agreed to check around for us. But, to our dismay, there was no room at the inn—anywhere! Not to worry—there were still many lovely bed & breakfasts in the area and she gave us the phone number of one close by. Cecil made the call. They were booked solid. She recommended another B & B, a short distance away. No vacancy. The hospitable proprietors passed us from one to another until finally we found a bed for the night. We had to travel several miles outside of the city, over winding back country roads before finding "Sally," her bed and breakfast parked in the middle of pastures dotted prolifically with fluffy white sheep—a true pastoral setting—peaceful and serene.

Darkness was falling as we met our hostess and were ushered to our room. Sally seemed a bit awkward, almost a novice at this task as she hurriedly completed our check-in. She had another family waiting, another alpha male who had also disdained making reservations, and who had literally followed us from the hotel to Sally's. Given the isolation of our accommodations, I was relieved that we were not the only guests for the night.

We had stayed in several B & B's over the years, warm cozy places, decorated with charming furnishings, resembling real homes. You couldn't quite squeeze Sally's B & B into that category. Although it was clean, the furnishings were spartan:

twin beds, a chair, table with lamp, and a bookcase graced with a few ponderous tomes holding each other up. The walls were bare; a throw rug decorated the tired linoleum floor. Our barely utilitarian bathroom adjoined our bedroom but you had to go back out in the hall to access it. At least it had a lock. Our bedroom door also had a lock but since the door didn't shut completely, it was merely decorative. What really set our room apart, however, was a mysterious door leading down to a dark place beneath the house. Yes, we checked it out. Unlocked doors are meant to be opened, aren't they? It might have been a basement, but our imaginations had kicked in by now, and we facetiously labeled it the "dungeon." Thankfully, the unlocked door leading to the dungeon was situated beside Cecil's bed— right next to his head.

Circumstances being a bit creepy, the tense atmosphere between us morphed into friendliness—we understood instantly that we needed to be on the same team. After saying good-night, I humorously whispered to Cecil, "This reminds me of a Stephen King novel," then promptly fell into a sound sleep and proceeded to sleep like a rock all night, protected by my strong, fearless hubby.

Cecil wasn't so fortunate. He tossed and turned restlessly most of the night. He suffered nightmares in which a mad psychopath with evil intent snuck up those back stairs wielding a butcher knife. He wrestled with the madman who was trying to drag him to the dungeon to torture and kill him.

I awakened refreshed, ready to enjoy my hubby and our anniversary. Cecil looked as if he really ***had*** been wrestling with a madman all night. I couldn't help but nervously chuckle as he recounted his night's adventures. We performed our morning ablutions, packed up, and gingerly approached the table for the "breakfast" part of B & B. The other guests joined us at the table as our congenial hostess served us coffee, juice, fresh fruit and some kind of unidentifiable muffins, right out of the oven. Besides the bottoms being burned, the muffins contained some grainy substance that I couldn't quite place. I cautiously sampled the muffin, quietly puzzling aloud to Cecil about its unusual flavor. I couldn't help myself. I jokingly whispered in Cecil's ear, "I wonder if it's arsenic." He's a brave man—not afraid of much, but I noticed he didn't eat his muffin, either.

We were happy to leave this peaceful rest stop, and headed north toward L.L.Bean for a little shopping. Mid-morning we stopped at a roadside diner for some real breakfast. Our waitress was an attractive but feisty redhead, thirty-something, who immediately began verbally sparring with Cecil. My hubby likes the ladies, and they like him, too. He wasn't nicknamed the "Dungaree Doll" in his sophomore year of high school (by the senior girls) for no reason. They enjoyed bantering with each other all through our meal. As we walked to the car, I remarked to Cecil, "Now, that's the kind of girl you should have married; somebody who would dish it right back at you."

Cecil linked his arm to mine, tugged me close and totally floored me by spontaneously replying, "God gave me the best wife I could have ever wanted. I was just too dumb to know it for a long time." And that after me almost killing him—twice—with my over-active imagination. Hmmm. Do you suppose I scared him into loving me?

We thoroughly enjoyed the rest of our weekend. He called ahead and made reservations for that night in Boston. We shopped and ate and enjoyed every moment of our time together. I carefully stored those precious words away in my heart and mind. They nourished me. When the marital seas get a little choppy, I pull them up on my mental computer monitor and am nourished again. They remind me of the Apostle Peter's words to the early believers . . . "Above all, love each other deeply, because love covers over a multitude of sins." I've been thankful for that verse many times through the years. Our marriage is the successful beneficiary of that beautiful truth.

Word Searches,
Mazes and Bingo

I was spending a significant amount of time babysitting for Daniel and Matthew, my two young grandsons. With the prospect of much more time together, (due to their mother's employment), I purchased a few tools of the trade, among them a book of mazes for four to six year olds to do with Matthew, and word searches for ages eight and up for Daniel.

One Wednesday morning, I sat on the couch, sandwiched between the two boys, focusing first on the right (Matthew), then on the left (Daniel). At first, Matthew was enthusiastically and diligently working on the easy mazes, but as they got increasingly more challenging, he began to lose interest (he was only three). He picked up a hand-held electronic game that his mother had just replaced the batteries in, and began an exciting blow-by-blow narration of his successful campaign, tantalizing his older brother who was still sitting by Nani [me] and doing boring old word searches.

Besides actually doing the word searches, however, the activity book also included intriguing facts about each page's unique topics, and some other fun activities. Daniel and I *had* been enjoying the "other" activities and had worked diligently on completing two or three of the word search puzzles. But with a stimulating—and loud—diversion occurring in the room, he, too, appeared to be losing interest as we started a page called, "Reptiles and Amphibians." We found a few obvious words, but with interest flagging, I suggested we make it a timed exercise, thinking my scholarly young grandson would be stimulated by that added requirement. We would each try to find two words off the list in about five minutes. Daniel and I were struggling and he began to be seriously distracted. I found *bullfrog*, then, *gecko*. Even though Daniel's focus had now shifted to the major stimulation taking place in the big chair next to him, I could see he was a bit bothered by my success, so I diplomatically addressed the problem.

I mentioned that the word search book was meant for ages eight and up. "Are you eight?" I asked.

"Yes," Daniel replied, then conscientiously qualified his answer with an "almost." (He would turn eight in two days).

"Well, I'm a lot older than eight," I said, "and you're better at these word searches than I am. I should be better than you are, don't you think, because I am *much* older." He solemnly agreed with me, as if that were a no-brainer. He didn't actually say the word, but the message came through . . . DUH!!

"I'm really smart," he said. But not wanting to sound too proud, or as if he were bragging, he quickly, once again, qualified his answer. "I'm as smart as an eight-year-old—and older," he added. Since Daniel has a naturally sensitive nature, he realized that I might feel a little inferior to his obvious prowess with words and superior intellect, and in an effort to soften the blow to my wounded ego, he magnanimously added, "But you're probably really good at bingo."

Dreams Divine; In-Betweens

Somewhere I read, (I think in one of Frederick Buechner's books), that the ancient Druids were fascinated by "in-betweens." For instance, mist that is neither rain nor air, or dreams that are a kind of consciousness manifested during sleep that is neither sleep, nor wakefulness.

Scientists tell us that everyone dreams—many times a night, even though we usually don't remember them. How real are dreams? What is the purpose of a dream? The Bible often records dreams that foretell important events e.g., Joseph's story in the Old Testament. Much of Native Americans' ideology was based on dreams. For me, though, dreams are elusive and vague, rarely premonitions of some future event, but, more likely, messages symbolizing some inner emotional crisis my conscious mind cannot deal with. Once, I dreamed I was driving a completely enclosed armored car through a crowd of people. Having just experienced a painful betrayal, it was easy to figure out why I had barricaded myself out of reach of everyone.

Occasionally I've dreamed that ants or gypsy moths were crawling all over me and leapt out of bed, wildly brushing off the non-existent critters. Those dreams occurred during major infestations of those very creatures, an obvious stimulus for my nighttime neurosis.

In the most vivid dream I can ever recall having about my beloved grandmother, she and I were walking together toward some dead or dying person. In the dream we knew who it was, but I couldn't see his or her face. So the identity of the person was both inexplicably known to me in my dream and not known to me in my wakefulness. I wondered aloud to Grandma about the mystery of death and, with genuine curiosity, I asked her, "What's it like to be dead?" She had been gone many years at that time.

She laughed, seemed to ponder her response then said, "It's lonely."

I was surprised by her answer. When I thought about it, though, I realized that as a mother she would not feel complete until all her children were gathered around her. Her answer made sense to me, making me wonder if those who depart miss those they leave behind with as much intensity as we miss them.

My most memorable dreams, however, revolved around some form of fear—fear of harm to one of my children, or fear of death. I once dreamed that I died. My youngest daughter was a mere two months old when I began experiencing some nasty pains in my side and other ominous symptoms. The doctor ordered several tests for gall bladder and ulcers. After two days of fasting, ingesting vile potions, and enduring several x-rays, they sent me home with no conclusive results. Although I still felt ill, I was applying a little eye makeup the next day when I noticed that the whites of my eyes were not white. I called the doctor and said, "I have yellow eyes."

"You'd better get right down here," he'd replied. They ran another round of tests—blood and urine this time and sent me home with this diagnosis: "You have hepatitis." Our home had to be quarantined and our entire household inoculated.

As I grew progressively more ill, my mother—always an angel of mercy—took off work to care for me, baby Sarah, and the rest of my household. Bed-bound, a couple of Job's comforters came to visit and solemnly offered their wisdom. Vic mournfully recounted how yellow his late wife had gotten just before she died of leukemia. Lon shared that a chronic itch plagued his father as he awaited death from cirrhosis of the liver. It didn't take any more than those ominous observations to tweak my vulnerable imagination. I was yellow—really yellow, and itching like crazy—so much so I had scratched myself almost raw. I called the doctor to report these dire symptoms. "Am I dying?" I queried.

He laughed and assured me my illness was not terminal.

But death was on my mind. I was only twenty-six years old, a wife and mother of two girls: a five-year-old and a baby. I didn't want to die. I probably scared my mother a bit as she came in my room one day, knelt by my bed, placed her hand on me and prayed for my healing. I prayed, too.

That night I dreamed I died. As is often the case with a powerful dream, the strong emotions awakened me. I laid there in a state of paralysis, likely fear-induced. I tried to lift my arms but they seemed to be weighted down. I couldn't move. I thought I was dead. I wept silently and fervently petitioned God. "Please, God, I don't want to die," I pleaded desperately. "I want to live." I don't know how long my spirit wrestled with God before eventually quieting.

In the silent stillness following a storm of tremendous ferocity, I heard a voice. Was it audible? I don't know. But it came through with clarity and tenderness. Only two words. Powerful words. "Trust me."

I knew that voice. "Yes, Lord," I answered aloud. "I trust You." I felt encompassed in love, safe, and at peace. I closed my eyes and slept.

The next morning when I awakened, I knew I was better. Much better. Healed. I got out of bed that day. Two days later my mother went home and I resumed my household duties. The wonder of that nocturnal mystical moment carried me through many challenges in the days and weeks ahead. Trust does not come easily to me. So many difficult life experiences corrupt our childlike trust. That one surreal moment of affirmation should have lasted me a lifetime. Unfortunately, I would find my faith fragile and faltering on several occasions during the journey ahead. But that's a story for another time.

Some dreams teach us lessons or reveal hidden messages to us. Often, they merely reflect what our conscious mind fears. When my girls were young, I would often suffer nightmares revolving around their safety. I would occasionally moan aloud or kick Cecil while in the midst of one of those terrifying dreams. One time, I was groaning and moaning heartily, helplessly mired in nightmare quicksand. Cecil, who had gone in the bathroom to pee, tried unsuccessfully to awaken me by calling my name several times, and had to "cut his leak short" so he informed me in exasperation as he shook me awake!

Cecil and I and Sarah, who was about six at the time, were enjoying a stroll down a pleasant pathway lined with trees when three big ferocious men appeared in my dream with us. They had evil intentions, that is, they planned to steal Sarah.

My hubby is the kind of man who thinks he's invincible. Even in my dream, I realized he figured he could take on all three of those monsters and he enthusiastically went right at them, fists flailing left and right. The odds weren't good, though, and this was my baby chick being threatened, too. I wanted to help. Somehow, I grabbed hold of a thick shock of black hair on the head of one of those nasty guys and pulled with every fiber of my being. I hung on tightly and tenaciously.

I was awakened abruptly by someone slapping my hand and angrily yelling, "Quit pulling my hair." You see, I had my hand in Cecil's hair and was pulling with all my might. I don't think he appreciated my help. He says that's why his hair is a little thin on top. It could be.

I had a dream, once, that seemed as if it were real life—a dream that brought resolution to an unfinished relationship. I had a dear friend named Cora. Everybody loved Cora. Not only was she attractive, she was a human dynamo with a cheerful countenance and positive attitude. Any function was a lot more fun if Cora was present. We had worked together amicably in the church in various capacities, without disagreement, competitiveness, jealousy or strife. After several years of friendship, a divisive third person entered the picture. Eventually, I felt betrayed by this person and Cora was deceived. A huge chasm grew between us—we remained friendly, but not really friends. Cora moved to Florida—a long way from Pennsylvania. The report came that Cora had a spot on her pancreas. I wrote her a letter expressing my belief in her and my love for her. She called me on the telephone, her voice strong, her attitude upbeat. She planned to conquer this foe. But the tests showed otherwise—Cora had pancreatic cancer and it had begun to spread. I sent her books and letters of encouragement. She called me twice more, at first still hoping for a miracle, but it was not to be. The last time I spoke with her, she had come to terms with her prognosis; even through the many miles that physically separated us, I sensed her spirit was calm and at peace.

I had sent Cora a copy of one of my very favorite books, *I Heard the Owl Call My Name* by Margaret Craven. The book tells the story of a young vicar, Mark, who is dying but doesn't know it. His bishop sends him to the poorest parish in his charge—a village of Kwakiutl Indians along the sea coast of British Columbia. One day, in the story, Mark, along with two of his parishioners, Jim and Keetah, trek upstream to see the end of the salmon, which they call the "swimmer." I don't know if Cora ever read the book but in my last letter to her I quoted the following sections . . . *"Under the clear water they saw the female swimmer digging the seed beds with her torn tail, her sides deep red and blue, her fins battered and worn . . . 'when she has laid her eggs and the waiting males have covered them with milt, she will linger, guarding them for several days,' Jim said . . . they moved again and saw the end of the swimmer. They watched her last valiant fight for life, her struggle to right herself when the gentle stream turned her, and they watched the water force open her gills and draw her slowly downstream, tail first, as she had started to the sea as a fingerling . . . in Keetah's eyes there were tears . . . 'the end of the swimmer is sad,' she said . . . 'But Keetah, it isn't. The whole life of the swimmer is one of courage and adventure. All of it builds to the climax and the end. When the swimmer dies he has spent himself completely for the end for which he was made, and this is not sadness. It is triumph." (pp. 49-50)*

I reminded Cora that of anyone I'd ever known, she fit that description—a life spent passionately, completely, fully engaged as intended by the Creator. Her life was a triumph.

I never saw Cora again—except—in my dream. One night, I dreamed that Cora was at my door—a full, solid clear glass door. Dressed, I believe, in a full-skirted, floor-length light blue gown, she was smiling at me with a loving expression on her face. She put both of her hands against the glass. I understood she wanted me to respond in like manner. When I lifted my hands and put them against the glass, instead of cold, hard glass, I felt warm living flesh. We stood facing each other, hands pressed together, with no barrier between us. The sensation was so real and vivid that it awakened me. I knew that Cora now knew the whole story and understood it fully. I believe she visited to reassure me of that and to communicate her love for me.

In between birth and death there exists a remarkable reality we call—Life. Is it more real than the before and/or after of our brief appearance on this planet? Is what we see and hear and touch more real than the invisible world existing around us?

In between sleep and wakefulness is also a reality called dreaming. Dreams can be many things: entertaining, or exhausting; reassuring, or frightening; clarifying, or confusing. They are in-between realities, but they are real, nevertheless.

I have periodically emotionally withdrawn from life to an in-between state, a kind of limbo—a daydream world that's not quite real—as a spectator to life, not fully engaged. It's safer there. Sometimes it appears to mean emotional survival or self-preservation of our fragile spirit. But it's not what God intended for the crown of His creation.

Living life openly with transparency is risky, often dangerous, messy or hurtful. It's rarely easy, neat and tidy. But it's better than the alternative. I once read an epitaph that went like this: *Besides was born and died, between she [fully] lived.* In a sense my life—all of our lives are "in-betweens." With all my heart I want my "in-between" to be relevant and efficacious. When my time here is over, I hope the essence of me will waft heavenward as a fragrant aroma to my Creator, and yet, linger in those I've poured myself into as a sweet indelible perfume.

Eternal Seeds

My daughter, Andrea, never seemed to have much of a green-thumb. Every plant she touched appeared to eventually end up brown and withered. Her sister was the one who had inherited their Grandmother's green-thumb. Sarah's various houseplants grew lush and green. I had started a Christmas cactus for both my girls from my plant—a fourth generation cactus that had originated from my Great Aunt Ida's. Sarah's bloomed beautifully all year, and was covered with buds and blossoms this December—sixty some at its peak, while Andrea's had died of neglect. The busyness of everyday living often made her feel as if she were traveling through life in the express lane, too fast to take care of three busy boys—her top priority, and plants, too.

Now my mother was gone. We all felt a strong inner compulsion to stay connected to her in our own ways. When we began sorting and dispersing various items of my mother's, I asked Andrea if she'd like her Grandmother's small dish garden as it had been a gift from her boys to their Great-Grandma on one of her many hospital stays. My mother had loved the dish garden of various plants with the replica of a bright red cardinal presiding majestically over it—a cardinal Andrea's eight-year-old son, Daniel, thoughtfully placed on his Great-Grandma's grave.

The dish garden, looking droopy and dejected, came to life for Andrea as she carefully nurtured it—as did the few other plants she had taken. All through the fall, winter and spring of the year following my mother's change of address, Andrea enjoyed watching the healthy resurrection of her new houseplants. Sometime in May, she decided to "branch out" and try her hand at some simple gardening—a few herbs and vegetables. She planted some basil and oregano around a couple of pepper plants in a large pot on the back deck. All she needed was a couple of tomato plants, but she kept forgetting to buy the seedlings or a pack of seeds.

One day Andrea sent her son, Sam, to Home Depot for a few necessary items for home repair. "Pick up a package of tomato seeds, too," she added, as he headed out the door.

When Sam returned, he pulled various items out of the bag: a container of screws; loose screening to re-screen the patio door; some all-purpose glue and a few other small items. She checked the bag—no tomato seeds. "Where's my tomato seeds, Sam?"

"Sorry, Mom," Sam replied to her question. "I forgot. Do you want me to go back?"

"No. Not today. I'll pick some up some day when I'm in town."

A few days later as Andrea was watering her plants, she noticed three tiny shoots growing among the plants in the dish garden. She wasn't sure but she thought they smelled like tomato plants when she leaned down for a closer look. When I stopped in later that day, she asked me to check out the dish garden. "Do you see those tiny seedlings? Are they tomato plants?" she excitedly asked me.

I looked intently and sniffed deeply. "Hmmm." Tomato plants have a wonderful distinctive aroma. "Yep. They're definitely tomato plants," I firmly asserted, sharing her excitement.

We knew that my mother, who had loved growing things, had planted tomato seeds every spring, including her last spring on earth. But her last spring was *an entire year ago*, now, and although she had planted a variety of plants, tomato seeds among them, (with the help of her friend, Estelle, my sisters Thelma and Jennie, and me) she had not planted any in the dish garden, already full of several bushy plants. The dish garden hadn't even set near the planters liberally sprinkled with tomato seeds.

A few weeks later, I reminded Andrea that she'd have to transplant those tender young plants. She carefully transplanted them into a large tub on the deck, fertilized and watered them. She and her family enjoyed watching them grow, feeling as if they had front row seats to a miracle in progress. When they grew tall, Andrea put a stake in the pot and tied them up. Soon small yellow blossoms appeared on the vines, followed shortly by tiny green tomatoes. The plants continued to thrive until frost threatened and she had to bring them in the house.

The tomato plant sat in front of the patio doors for the next few months, right alongside its "mother plant," my mother's dish garden. Green tomatoes grew in various stages throughout the fall, until eventually Andrea harvested nine succulent bright red tomatoes that she and her boys enjoyed eating all the way into the dark month of December. They all liked tomatoes but these tomatoes tasted especially sweet. Going through a challenging time in her life, she knew they were a special gift to her—a personal reminder that she was not alone, forgotten or unloved.

As a young girl, the greatest desire of my mother's heart had been to become a missionary when she grew up. Instead, she got married and had seven children. So she planted seeds of faith in those seven fertile receptacles and tenderly nurtured them. Although she loved planting flowers and vegetables, my mother's most rewarding crops were those fragile, almost imperceptible seeds she liberally, lovingly sowed in the lives of her various offspring—seeds of honesty, tolerance, industry, kindness, hope, faith and, most of all, love. Her seeds always produced a good harvest, apparently even from the other side.

The indigenous "first peoples" in this country we call America believed that we should be preparing our offspring for the future—planning seven generations ahead. Somehow, I know, my mother's seeds will continue to grow healthy and fruitful in those who come after me.

My mother was intensely proud of her Native American blood (her great-grandmother was a full-blood Lenni/Lenape) and I included this anonymous poem, often attributed to Mary Elizabeth Frye but possibly based on a Native American prayer, at her funeral:

Do not stand at my grave and weep,

I am not there, I do not sleep.

I am a thousand winds that blow,

I am the diamond glints on snow,

I am the sunlight on ripened grain,

I am the gentle autumn rain,

I am the stars that shine at night.

When you awaken in the mornings hush,

I am the swift uplifting rush

Of quiet birds in circled flight.

Do not stand at my grave and cry,

I am not there, I did not die.

I'm not at all surprised that she's still industriously planting seeds!

Hidden Objects

"What time should I expect you in the morning?" I asked Sarah, referring to when she planned to drop off Elizabeth for the day. Elizabeth's school was having a teacher-in-service day so she didn't have school and would be spending the day with me.

"Let's say 9:15," my daughter said, "I have to be at class on time tomorrow." Sarah teaches two classes at the local community college and had cancelled her morning class the previous day because of weather related complications.

Elizabeth arrived at 9:35 a.m.—close to on time. Although she was dressed, she had not yet eaten, and was starving, of course—always. She settled in front of the TV, waiting for her faithful servant to prepare her requested breakfast and deliver it expeditiously—which I did. She didn't dawdle over breakfast, however, because we had lots of plans for the day, first and foremost being to head for the mall to get her a new winter coat. Elizabeth was wearing last year's coat and since she had grown considerably, the coat was too small. I figured the winter clothes would be on sale as the season was half over and we'd get a good buy on a coat. I was actually right about that.

"Can you sit in the front seat, yet?" I asked her. Although I pick her up at school two days a week, she still sits in the back. But she's tall and a month shy of ten; a shopping trip seemed to require different, more relaxed rules. (Uh-oh. I sound like my rule-resistant hubby—now that's a scary thought.)

"Oh, yes," she replied. "I weigh 105 pounds now and you only have to be 95 lbs."

"Are you sure?" I query. "Do you ever sit in the front with your mother?"

"Well, ummm, she lets me sometimes but usually she, ummm, has too much stuff in the front seat."

"What about your daddy? Does he ever let you sit in the front seat?"

"Well, sometimes. But he usually, ummm, has stuff in the front seat, too."

"Hmmm. Daniel sits in the front seat," I murmur, pondering this situation. Daniel won't be ten until July but he's a big guy—tall and stocky.

"Okay," I decide, "you can sit in front." (A premature decision as she actually weighed only 86 lbs. and the guidelines for sitting in the front seat are all over the place—from nine years to sixteen and 70 lbs. to the weight of a 165 lb. mature male—the size of a person manufacturers considered to safely survive if airbags were deployed.) We settle in, buckle up and are ready to go. I share a smile with my lovely granddaughter. "I like this; it seems friendlier. Just remember Nani's one major rule—you are not to ever disappear from my sight when we're shopping, okay? You stick to me like glue." I always worry because Elizabeth has been known to explore interesting stimuli outside your line of vision.

Our mall only has three modest department anchors and we hit the Bon-Ton first. Their ad in the newspaper flier advertised all kid's outer wear at huge discounts. The problem—they only had two coats in her size. "Ewwww," she immediately and very emphatically said, "not that one. A girl in my class has that coat." I could understand that reasoning. I'd bought a beautiful lavender coat for myself several years prior, then promptly bumped into ladies wearing the same coat everywhere I went. Not only that, they were all little old gray-haired ladies and I wasn't quite mentally ready to wear the uniform of the "senior class."

The only other possibility—a shiny fuchsia coat, fit a little too snugly. "Let's wait and check the other stores first. We can come back to this one if we have to." Elizabeth liked this coat but was amenable to checking around first.

Between the Bon-Ton and JC Penney we pass a plethora of stores. Elizabeth admires various items along the way. "Can we stop here, Nani?" she asks.

"After we get your coat," I tell her, watching her star-filled eyes trying to absorb all the wonders of retail. She doesn't get to go shopping too often and is overwhelmed with the abundant selections. Plus, there is thirty dollars burning a hole in her wallet and too many things to choose from.

As we're hurrying down the hall, we bump into Oma Doris, an "adopted" grandmother of Elizabeth's. We share hugs around and briefly discuss our plans for the day, then hurry on our way. When you're planning to spend money, nothing can distract you for long.

JC Penney had nothing—nada—at least not in coats. Not to worry though, they had an impressive girls' department and Elizabeth saw one or two things she liked. "I need some jeans," she said. "I love these jeans. Don't you love these jeans? Oh,

Nani, look at this shirt. It's so cool. Can I get this shirt? I need some new underwear, too. Mine are all too small. They hurt my bum." Everywhere we look she sees something she likes. We are smack dab in the middle of retail wonderland. "I don't want to be cute," Elizabeth informs me, "I want to be cool." We choose several pair of jeans, half a dozen "cool" shirts, and a couple of matching sets and head for the dressing room.

Elizabeth begins the tedious task of trying on clothes with her first choice—a cool outfit, stretch black capris with a matching multi-colored top and a bright spring green beaded necklace. It's too small. That's why you bring your personal servant along. While she peels the outfit off, I scurry out of the dressing room to search for a larger size. As Elizabeth tries on the next size, I retrieve the discarded clothes, which are inside out in a clump on the bench, turn them right side and carefully replace them on the hanger—a process repeated umpteenth times over the next hour. My last trip to find a different size, I see a blur out of the corner of my eye as Elizabeth dashes out of the dressing room, too, then quickly back in. When I return, she is dressed in a sleeveless white dress with a chiffon overskirt—a very fancy dress from the vast selection, strategically placed just outside the entrance to the girls' fitting room. She's sitting on the bench smiling hopefully up at me, her whole demeanor reflecting an obvious non-verbal question mark. I might have said "Yes" if the dresses were not, in my opinion, all so tacky but I shake my head "no" and she doesn't argue. When we're finally finished, she has three new pair of jeans, five "cool" shirts, a "snazzy" outfit, one dressy outfit with two exchangeable tops, a small shawl, and some underwear—but no coat!

As we head for the checkout, an angel disguised as a kind saleslady asks me if I'd like a coupon for 15 percent off. Since I'd planned on a coat—on sale—and, perhaps, a couple pair of jeans, I gratefully accepted her offer.

We head for Sears. "Oh, Nani, I love this store," Elizabeth gushes as we pass a specialty shop for young girls. "Can we go in?"

"After we look for a coat," I firmly reply in my no-nonsense voice, never breaking my brisk stride. I am just so much fun to shop with.

Sears has two coats in her size. She hones in on one—a bright pink coat with black and white accents. It fits perfectly, as a coat should—just a tiny bit big. While I'm checking to make sure there is not another option, she grabs a shirt off the rack and disappears into the fitting room. "Doesn't this shirt look nice, Nani?" she asks, smiling winsomely at me. "Can I get it? Please?"

"Okay, but that's it. Whatever else you want now, you're going to have to use your own money." I hurry us to the check-out before she can see anything else she loves, only to stand in line forever. Elizabeth peruses the merchandise in the immediate area. There are a few toys and she still has that thirty dollars of her own to spend. She picks up a bright yellow stuffed "Pikachu" pillow.

"Oh, Nani, I love this pillow. Daniel has one just like it. I could sleep with it at my dad's." Elizabeth is hugging it tightly. "Can I get it, Nani?"

"I don't know, Elizabeth. Remember you want to go back to that shop with all the pretty girl stuff? What would your mother say?" Elizabeth is torn—she wants it but she's not sure how her mother will feel. And, she still wants to stop in that other shop. While we're waiting in line, I visit with Sarah's best friend, Denise, from high school, Denise's two little boys, and her mom, Karen. They're waiting to pick up pictures from the Sears portrait studio. I introduce Elizabeth to Denise and her mom; Elizabeth reminds Denise of Sarah both in looks, and actions, as Elizabeth spontaneously makes a funny comment, which makes her laugh. Denise tells me that I haven't changed at all; I haven't seen her in ten, maybe fifteen years. I am momentarily energized by that comment. If I look forty-five instead of sixty, I should be able to shop till I drop.

The customer in front of us has a problem. After waiting in line about ten minutes, another sales lady sends us downstairs to check out. Together, the $60.00 dollar coat, on sale for $24.99, and the "snazzy" shirt tally $17. 98. The coat only cost $9.00 dollars! What a huge blessing.

We have to pass the small food court on our way back. It's past noon and Elizabeth is hungry. "Can we get something to eat?" she asks. At my affirmative nod she continues, "I want a foot long sandwich from Subway."

"A foot long," I exclaim in disbelief. "You can't eat that much."

"Daddy and I always eat those," she says with certainty.

I agree to a Subway sandwich—but only half of one. I give her some money and sit at a seat close as she goes and orders her own. She runs back to me, "I need another dollar." Again, she hurries to me. "Bacon is extra. Can I have another dollar?" One more time Elizabeth needs more money. "Can I get an iced tea?"

She sees a girl she knows from chorus and they exchange greetings. As we're leaving the food court, Elizabeth stops to admire her chorus friend's baby brother and we briefly chat with her mom—a warm, friendly moment in our day.

As we're headed back to the specialty girl's shop, I have to periodically nudge Elizabeth along—there is so much interesting stuff to see.

I'm supposedly done spending. Elizabeth knows she must spend her own money now. She thoughtfully peruses the merchandise. She wants to spend her own money on something special. I suggest she get some hair accessories and she chooses two hair bands to match her new outfits.

She vacillates on various items when her eye spies some sparkly items displayed along the wall. There is no question, no hesitation as she heads for the glitter—hightop sneakers, covered in silver sequins. Elizabeth's doubts are over. She has found exactly what her heart desired—something totally cool and fashionable.

At the check-out she begins to stress once again. "Maybe I shouldn't get them," she ponders aloud. "What will Mommy think?" Elizabeth's distress is palpable and I reassure her all will be fine. However, she does not have enough money. As we weigh the decision—to buy, or not to buy based on her finances—the sales clerk pulls out a 40 percent off coupon. Angels are everywhere on this shopping expedition. The $60 plus tab is reduced to $32.00! Elizabeth puts ten of her thirty dollars on the counter. In business you'd call that maneuver the "assumptive close." She's an expert closer. Guess who pays the balance? I qualify for a halo and wings, too. I let her wear her new coat and sneakers, and she walks proudly to the car. Sometimes all it takes to feel momentarily reborn is a new pair of shoes—and her feet were twinkling and shining like the stars.

As we leave the mall, Elizabeth asks, "Can we stop at Aunt Andrea's?"

I call Andrea on my cell phone to see if it's okay. We spend a few minutes there, long enough for Elizabeth to show off her beautiful sneakers and "mother" her five-year-old cousin, Matthew, by getting him dressed and combing his hair. Her Aunt Andrea, once a consummate shopper, too, admires Elizabeth's stylish footwear, remembering some snazzy shoes she wore in her teen years.

Elizabeth is still a bit anxious as she models her new shoes for her mother a short time later. "Are you mad?" she asks her mother.

"They're not very practical, but why should I be mad?" Sarah asks. She humorously adds, "I didn't have to pay for them."

My initial plans for our day together included making popcorn balls and finishing reading a book Elizabeth and I were working on—besides buying a new coat, that is. The best laid plans often don't materialize as we visualized. My pocketbook was considerably thinner at the end of the day, but my heart got a fresh infusion of healthy nutrients via Elizabeth's total engagement in every facet of her day—shopping for new clothes, of course, an adrenalin rush for most girls. But Elizabeth noticed people, too, and touched them with her innate warmth as we encountered them along our path throughout the day. And as we interacted with those various people, we were blessed to be the recipients of various acts of kindness.

I enjoyed seeing a glimmer in Elizabeth of her great-aunt Jennie, my eldest sister, who lives far away in Hawaii and who passionately embraces life and who loves to shop, too. But I also saw a bit of her Aunt Andrea in her—Andrea, who besides enjoying shopping trips, also never complained as she worked on the task at hand, but steadily and cheerfully plugged away. And, although her mother, Sarah, hated shopping at Elizabeth's age (and still does), her mother's fingerprints were visible all over her as she warmly interacted with all those God brought across our path—just as her mother did wherever we might be.

I am filled with new hope for the future after a day spent shopping with Elizabeth. Our day together was filled with both big and little blessings, reminding me that in the midst of a world saturated with hate and violence, pain and heartache, selfishness and suffering, love is quietly, consistently, resolutely still hard at work. Often we measure goodness by selfless acts of great heroism. I believe that finding goodness in our daily mundane lives is a much greater challenge.

Goodness, according to my Oxford thesaurus, is a broad word describing "an excellence so well established that it is thought of as inherent or innate and is associated with kindness, generosity, helpfulness and sincerity." I'm fond of "hidden object" games on my computer, and recognizing those almost imperceptible, invisible, seemingly insignificant moments of "salt" and "light" amongst the cluttered debris of a normal day is a true "hidden object" quest with a satisfying "win"—a "win" called authentic goodness.

It was a very good day.

Wings to Fly

Scritch. Scrrrriiitch. Scritch. I shook my head groggily. "Whatever is that sound?" I wondered. I lifted my head off the pillow, straining to hear, but there was only silence. Probably nothing. I must have been dreaming. *Scritch. Scritch. Scrrrriiitch.* Pause. *Scrrriiitch. Scritch. Scritch.* Alarmed, and now wide awake, I reached over to pat my hubby. He wasn't there. I looked at the clock—4 a.m. Then my mind engaged. I stumbled out of bed and opened the door to the den that adjoins our bedroom, stuck my head around it and with humorous exasperation said, "Okay. You called your first turkey for the day." It was the first day of spring gobbler season, and my excited hubby was fully dressed in camouflage ready to take to the woods, and diligently practicing his turkey call with his "box" call. Obviously, he's a highly skilled turkey caller. He hadn't even left the house and he'd already called in his trophy. Well, maybe not a trophy but a very large hen turkey, for sure! (My apologies to any turkey hunters who can't comprehend my attempt at duplicating the sound that little box actually makes.)

Although we live just on the outskirts of town, we see more wildlife than I ever recall seeing when I truly lived in a more rural area of Pennsylvania as a child and young adult. Besides the ubiquitous whitetail deer, we've had black bears, coyotes, woodchucks, skunks, raccoons, opossums, rabbits, foxes, squirrels and turkeys parading around our yard at various times. Some of them hardly qualify for the classification of "wild" as they need to be shooed away innumerable times before they leave the premises—only to return a short time later. Next to whitetail deer, turkeys are the worst offenders. Looking for birdseed, they'll nonchalantly take a stroll on our back deck, as if it were home, occasionally depositing a little lump of leftovers for our enjoyment.

Several years ago, my hubby decided to try his hand at gardening. With my mother's dedication to the craft, she had often planted small vegetable patches which attracted a variety of those scavenging wild critters. Cecil knew he'd have to take some serious measures to thwart those backyard invaders. Not only did he fence the area, he enclosed it with a six foot high barrier mesh fence, and much to the chagrin of our girls, he even added a screen door, which listed slightly to the side and flapped in the breeze if inadvertently left unlatched. It might have made perfect sense, but it kinda resembled the stereotypical hillbilly compound. All that was missing was some moonshine, a weary hound dog, and a dilapidated outhouse!

Mid-summer, we would often see two hen turkeys parading through our yard, a queue of little turkeys following behind. We enjoyed watching them grow, although the line invariably began to shrink—the tender toddlers falling victim to one of the many prowling predators.

One day, as I was working in my kitchen, I heard some serious clucking going on in the backyard. I'm not sure how it managed to get in this predicament, but a lone toddling turkey was running back and forth, back and forth inside our hillbilly compound, desperately searching for the exit. Except for one concerned Mama, the rest of the family had moved on. Mama turkey was talking nonstop to her errant child, clucking encouragement from outside of the fence. I watched this backyard drama with fascination for several minutes, silently rooting for their success, but they were unable to find any resolution to their dilemma. Toddling turkey couldn't find his or her way out and Mama turkey had not found the right words to motivate her offspring to conquer the challenge. They seemed to be at a stalemate.

Time for some supernatural help and "Superwoman Lela" carefully opened the back door. The anxious clucking immediately turned to frantic squawking and the two turkeys noticeably increased their pace. Back and forth they scurried frenetically as I slowly inched my way toward the garden. Normally, I'd be chasing these critters, yelling and flapping my arms like a wild woman, just to get them to move. But this was new territory—threatening territory—outside their control, and they were terrified of me, not realizing that I planned to be their savior. When I stepped off the deck, Mama frantically uttered the magic words, and toddler turkey furiously flapped his own wings, caught the air current and fluttered awkwardly, but successfully, up and over the fence and into the nearby woods to safety. Fear accomplished what Mama's encouragement could not. I understood that motivation; I'd experienced a similar situation many years earlier.

About a year after Cecil's fledgling building business began to show some life, we relocated to the area, and, thankfully, he replaced his lone inept assistant [me] with more proficient employees. Although I would eventually be called "the phantom" due to my invisibility, I frequently stopped in during the early years.

One afternoon, after I picked my daughter Sarah up from school, she and I drove the short distance to the office. Cecil's office was located, at the time, in the former garage/basement of a cape-cod-styled real estate office just off the interstate—a good location. The driveway sloped down along the side of the building, bounded on one side by a small strip of untended land, and on the other by a stone wall that gradually increased in height until reaching several feet above my head. I'm five feet, six inches tall so the wall was likely about eight feet high where it joined the building. A well maintained yard graced the front of the building with a few trees scattered about, and right next to the building, just above the stone wall, a cluster of evergreens grew thick and fragrant. A generous parking area to the left of the yard accommodated visitors and employees alike and I parked my car there.

One of life's sweetest pleasures, I believe, is walking with a little person, their small hand clasped trustingly in yours. Sarah, a precocious six-year-old at the time, rarely walked anywhere when she was little—she ran. I remember warning her when she was only three about the potential hazards of running down our driveway at home—a long, steep, winding and bumpy red shale road. "Be careful. You might fall and get hurt," I'd utter cautiously.

"I want my hair to get fatter," she replied in sheer delight on one of those occasions. Her light, fluffy hair floated around her head, moved by the breeze, giving her a false sense of fullness in her hair as she fearlessly ran down the driveway, in spite of my dire warnings.

Her older sister, Andrea, never needed to be warned—she innately feared falling. As a toddler, she'd walk around the house moving from one stationary object to another, holding on for dear life. In fact, she could carry on a logical and coherent conversation with you before she finally let go of the furniture. If you asked her why she wouldn't let go, she didn't hesitate to respond clearly and succinctly, "I'll fall down." Duh! As if anyone with a brain didn't know that.

Anyway, on this day, as Sarah and I began our descent to the office, she abruptly dropped my hand and raced off, disappearing into the group of evergreen trees above the stone wall. I continued walking, while issuing orders to my mischievous daughter. "Sarah, you come here. Right now. I mean it."

A smiling little face peeked out from behind a tree. Unfazed by my stern orders, she waved and said, "Hi Mommy." Her happy face turned to one of surprise, as she inexplicably disappeared, the ground opening up beneath her feet.

It sounds incredible—even to me—but I believe I sprouted wings and flew up over that wall. Or, perhaps, I was lifted on the wings of an angel. However I got there—it was as fast as a blink of the eye. Sarah was desperately clinging with her small fingers and all her might to the uneven rim of an old well, the dirt and debris still raining on her frightened little face. I didn't think—I just reacted, reaching down and lifting her to safety. Pine needles had camouflaged an old rotten wooden board that covered a well—thankfully dry, but still deep enough to have caused Sarah considerable physical harm, and created challenges in retrieving her had she fallen to the bottom. As I write these words about that brief but terrifying moment in time, I can still feel the talons of my own huge fear gripping me tightly.

Cecil had customers with him when we entered the office. Other than being covered with flecks of dirt, rotten wood and pine needles, Sarah seemed fine. I couldn't stop trembling, however, and Cecil's customers thought I needed something—a shot of whiskey was their recommendation. But I was fine, too; my baby girl was safe.

I've often pondered that surreal fleeting moment. I will never know—at least in this life—how exactly I got "in the twinkling of an eye" from point A to point B. I'm absolutely certain of this one thing—I did *not* run back up the driveway and through the yard to reach my precious little girl.

Much of our life is ruled by fear—a cheapening, constricting kind of fear: fear of punishment, ridicule, rejection, failure, exposure, danger or pain. In some cases it may actually work to our benefit—but it is rarely a pleasant experience. Apparently, however, there is a kind of fear that's a good fear—a fear that gives us strength to do the seemingly impossible—whether you're a toddler turkey or a fallible human. I know the source of my strength—and I'm thankful . . . *But those who hope in the Lord will renew their strength. They will soar on wings like eagles, they will run and not grow weary, they will walk and not be faint (Isa. 40:31).*

Conclusion:
The Bear, the Lamb,
the Lion

My husband is an avid hunter. Over the many years of our marriage, he's taken innumerable hunting trips for a variety of game, about a dozen of which adorn the walls of our family room. It takes a little getting used to—all those glassy eyes staring unrelentingly at you. I dress them up at Christmas with bright red bows and bells, the only time they look as if they're enjoying their lot in life.

I see myself as a peacemaker, not exactly gentle as a lamb, but definitely with passive-aggressive tendencies rather than overt assertiveness. I persistently pursue peace, as the apostle Peter suggests, but the process often involves the dreaded confrontation, which I do not enjoy and try my best to avoid.

Several years ago I purchased a stuffed toy—a black bear, not a teddy bear but an authentic replica of a real black bear. About the size of an adult housecat, I placed it on our bed for decoration. It looked as if it belonged there.

Somewhere I also found an adorable lamb—kind of like a fat Humpty Dumpty with a round body, a little head, and four dangling appendages.

During one of my husband's seriously unhappy phases, I whimsically decided to re-position the bear, placing him on his butt in the corner of a bench in our bedroom. I moved the lamb, too, into the waiting arms of the black bear. The arms of the bear enfold the lamb around the middle, holding the lamb's arms, which I have carefully uplifted, in place. Since the lamb is a lady (me, in this case), I politely cross those spindly stick legs at the ankles. To a casual observer, it appears the bear (Cecil) is hugging the lamb. At times that might be true. But, when I united these two critters, the lamb was calling, "Help! Rescue me," because it appeared she [I] was about to become dinner for a fierce, dangerous and ravenous predator [Cecil]. It was my own "sweet" way of getting even with my hubby and saying, "Take that, you big bully." It tickled my fancy enough that I decided to leave them that way. Cecil walked past that symbolic tableau several times a day without ever realizing the drama it represented.

The day came, however, when I felt comfortable sharing the meaning of that little scene with my hubby. Thankfully, he laughed. Then, he put his take on the scene. "Wait a minute," he said. "I think the bear is holding up the lamb's arms so it can win the battle, just like Moses," referring to a story in the Bible. (Trust a man to make himself the hero. I may be winning but only because he's either letting me or helping me). *As long as Moses held up his hands, the Israelites were winning, but whenever he lowered his hands, the Amalekites were winning. When Moses' hands grew tired, they took a stone and put it under him and he sat on it. Aaron and Hur held his hands up— one on one side, one on the other—so that his hands remained steady until sunset. So Joshua overcame the Amalekite army with the sword* (Exod. 17:11-13).

"Or, perhaps," I added thoughtfully, "the lamb with arms uplifted is fervently praising the Lord."

The lamb may be crying out for deliverance, or praising the Lord; she may be receiving strength, security and support from the big bear, or, more likely, the bear is holding the lamb just to hold her—providing warmth, and comfort and love, a place we all yearn to call home. Whatever the lamb is doing, she is doing it still. Except, there are occasions . . . whenever my mature social worker/professor daughter Sarah has been in my bedroom for some reason, I'll find my poor little lamb turned upside down, its head buried beneath its wide butt which is sticking straight up. I'm not sure what symbolism to attach to that picture.

You may think I'm a pathetic coward because I prefer to live a peaceful co-existence instead of a constantly confrontational one. The following words taken from a beautiful book, *The Lakota Way* by Joseph M. Marshall III, resonate profoundly with me . . . *Therefore, when resistance ceased to be an option, surviving within the parameters of white control on the reservations was the only choice. There was no other option but to reach deep inside and persevere day in and day out, year in and year out, from one generation to the next . . . [when the Lakota] could no longer defend themselves on the field of battle . . .they fought with the only weapon at their disposal: spiritual strength.* And that is exactly how my inner spirit has survived. I do not believe I am diminished as a person of validity by choosing to turn the other cheek, forgive the seemingly unforgivable or tolerate the intolerable. I know who I am and I even like me. I have not sacrificed my ideals nor compromised my identity. Besides, we can't all be alpha males, can we? We'd annihilate each other in no time flat.

Much of life is comprised of heartache, pain, injustice, and sometimes downright ugliness. Believing in a good God is often hard. I like how Philip Yancey once described the journey of faith—that God seems to like faith best in the fog. I've spent considerable time wandering around aimlessly on this faith walk, trying to see, wanting clearly defined markers to guide me. But you don't need faith if you can see where you're going. Faith trusts in the unseen navigator. (I know, there's that most difficult word in our vocabulary—trust.) But, when we really, really want something in life, we'll work at it, we'll do whatever it takes, we'll practice, practice, practice. Although faith is a gift, it takes effort and practice to be viable.

Complaining about all the hard things to my daughter, Sarah, one day, I immediately qualified my musings by mentioning the blessings, too. It's amazing, but sometimes your kids actually make sense. She said, "Well, then, if you connect all the dots of blessings, you'll have a beautiful picture." She's right. In the fabric of our everyday life, we can find numerous glimpses of goodness and redemption—if we look. Life is a beautiful blessing. Not the stuff we acquire, the clutter of tangible things that money can buy. Simple, un-adorned, naked life is a masterpiece made up of thoughts and feelings. We have been given a will to choose, a mind to think and wonder, and a heart to love. What a priceless gift! If only I'd embrace that gift instead of so often stooping to petty, self-absorbed poor me mentality.

I added—"the lion"—to the title for a reason. You often hear the phrase, "and the lion will lay down with the lamb," quoted as if it's Scripture. But it is not found in the Bible. Jesus, however, *is* referred to as both lion and lamb, that is, He's the

"Lamb of God, who takes away the sin of the world" and the "Lion of the tribe of Judah . . . [who] has triumphed." And, Isaiah 65 depicts a new heaven and a new earth where the wolf and the lamb and the lion are all co-habitating peacefully—where pain and sorrow and danger do not exist.

The picture, then, of the bear and the lamb living in harmony is a symbolic picture of the ideal world; when the King of the animal world—the lion—will reign with mercy and perfect justice, forever. My whimsical tableau is a prophetic picture of what could be, or should be, and ultimately will be. It is the final redemption. And so, I echo these words of the apostle John in the final pages of our Holy Book, "Blessed be the Lord, God Almighty, who is, and who was, and who is to come . . . Amen. Come, Lord Jesus."

Questions for Reflection and Discussion

1. Can you have authentic faith if you don't use it, that is, is there such a thing as inactive faith? How does faith "grow up?"

2. What qualities do we naturally have that often causes us to resist direction—even from God? Why do we have so much trouble submitting to authority as Matthew frequently demonstrates, e.g., "Time: Watching and Waiting"?

3. What qualities should a follower of Jesus always demonstrate? Never? Find examples where I got it right or wrong.

4. The apostle Paul writes that we need to think about the right things—things that are true and noble, for instance. He also tells us that, as believers, we actually have the mind of Christ and the ability to take our thoughts captive and make them obedient to Christ. Our minds can get us into a lot of trouble if we give them free reign. Throughout my journey of faith, my mind has created all kinds of faulty assumptions. Find two examples in the book. Think of a situation in your life that is comparable.

5. Why were so many of my prayers unanswered—or were they?

6. Is it easier for you to forgive a wrong done to you—or one done by you?

7. Peter writes, specifically to women, in his first epistle, "([your beauty] should be that of your inner self, the unfading beauty of a gentle and quiet spirit . . .") When you evaluate yourself as a person, what measuring stick are you using, that is, what mirror are you looking in? Is God's love your mirror? Your spouse or child or parent?

8. Look at the various "Bethel moments" in the stories—the times when the invisible reality and the tangible one overlapped ("Sept 12th, 2001", "A Tap on My Shoulder", "The Handle", "Insulin and Angels", "Looking, but not Seeing", "Call the Doctor", "Eternal Seeds", "Wings to Fly"). I believe those moments are manifestations of divine origin—for a specific purpose, perhaps gentle reminders that God's eyes and ears are attentive to our needs. Think of a "Bethel moment" in your life. Do you know why it occurred? If you can't recall one of those moments, is it possible you were distracted by other things and failed to notice. Find several "Bethel moments" in Scripture. What was the purpose?

9. How do you decide where to draw the line between giving up and persevering in relationship with a significant other? Do you have more tolerance for a parent? Child? Sibling? Friend? Are you able to see the challenges as opportunities for inner growth, or merely trials to endure with patience or longsuffering?

10. What "tools" do we utilize to sift through the clutter of an ordinary day to find the hidden gems of goodness? How pivotal is our personality type in viewing the challenges of life? Does faith in God affect/alter our perspective? How about a sense of humor?

11. How often do we pray that God will change others or deliver us from our difficult circumstances, rather than concentrating on what He might possibly want us to learn or change about ourselves?

12. Proverbs reminds us that "pride goes before destruction." What kind of pride is good pride? Can you be both proud and humble at the same time?

13. How have you seen God bring beauty from ashes, laughter from tears, hope from despair? What habits can you or have you developed to create those realities in your life?

14. Everybody has their own pain—it's just expressed in different ways. How does Cecil express his inner pain? How do I? How do you?

15. Do you believe that suffering in this life is inevitable? Why or why not? Do you accept it or fight against it?

16. There is an old hymn, "It will be worth it all, when we see Jesus . . ." At the end of the day you may ask yourself, "Was it worth it?" What will God say about me at the end of my day? What has God gotten out of His investment in my life?

17. Proverbs 3:12a states . . . "the Lord disciplines those he loves . . ." What purpose does discipline serve? Have you ever felt corrected by the God of the universe?

18. For most of my life, my mother was my "safe place." What qualities need to be present for you to confide your deepest thoughts and feelings in another? Is God enough?

19. Some form of fear is a highly motivating factor in many of my stories. When is fear a good thing? What delineates constructive fear from destructive? Find examples of various kinds of fear in the book.

20. We all worship something or someone. It may be obvious—fame, money, physical beauty or intellect; or it may be subtle—our personal pain or martyrdom, for instance. Who or what is the god you worship? How much time, thought and energy do you invest in that god?

**Intermedia
Publishing Group**

Publishing That Works For You

Do you need a speaker?

Do you want Lela Buchanan to speak to your group or event? Then contact Larry Davis at: (623) 337-8710 or email: ldavis@intermediapr.com or use the contact form at: www.intermediapr.com.

Whether you want to purchase bulk copies of *Finding Redemption In Everyday Life* or buy another book for a friend, get it now at: www.imprbooks.com.

If you have a book that you would like to publish, contact Terry Whalin, Publisher, at Intermedia Publishing Group, (623) 337-8710 or email: twhalin@intermediapub.com or use the contact form at: www.intermediapub.com.